Kaplan Publishing are constantly fin[ding] ways to make a difference to you[r studies and our] exciting online resources really do offer something different to students looking for exam success.

This book comes with free MyKaplan online resources so that you can study anytime, anywhere. **This free online resource is not sold separately and is included in the price of the book.**

Having purchased t[he]   [mat]erials:

CONTENT

Electronic version of the

Progress tests with insta[nt]

Mock assessments onlin[e]

Material updates

How to access your

Kaplan Financial studer[t]   be available to
you online. You do not r   d. If you are having
problems accessing onl[ine]

If you are not studying [with]   lock your extra online
resources please go to [d registered books
previously). You will the   the unique pass key
number contained in th[additional information
during this process to se[t u]

If you purchased through Ka[ll automatically receive
an e-mail invitation to MyKa[your content. If you do
not receive the e-mail or bo[o

Your Code and Informat[

This code can only be used on[your online content will
expire when the final sittings [ase allow one hour from
the time you submit your book

Please scratch the film to access your MyKaplan code.

Please be aware that this code is case-sensitive and you will need to include the dashes within the passcode, but not when entering the ISBN. For further technical support, please visit www.MyKaplan.co.uk

KAPLAN

PUBLISHING

INDIRECT TAX

STUDY TEXT

Qualifications and Credit Framework

AQ2016

Finance Act 2018

For assessments from 1 January to 31 December 2019

This Study Text supports study for the following AAT qualifications:

AAT Advanced Diploma in Accounting – Level 3

AAT Advanced Certificate in Bookkeeping – Level 3

AAT Advanced Diploma in Accounting at SCQF – Level 6

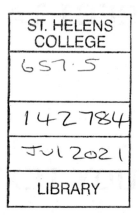
British Library Cataloguing-in-Publication Data

A catalogue record for this book is available from the British Library.

Published by
Kaplan Publishing UK
Unit 2, The Business Centre
Molly Millars Lane
Wokingham
Berkshire
RG41 2QZ

ISBN 978-1-78740-267-6

The text in this material and any others made available by any Kaplan Group company does not amount to advice on a particular matter and should not be taken as such. No reliance should be placed on the content as the basis for any investment or other decision or in connection with any advice given to third parties. Please consult your appropriate professional adviser as necessary. Kaplan Publishing Limited and all other Kaplan group companies expressly disclaim all liability to any person in respect of any losses or other claims, whether direct, indirect, incidental, consequential or otherwise arising in relation to the use of such materials.

Printed and bound in Great Britain

The Indirect Tax Reference material in the Appendix to this textbook has been supplied by the Association of Accounting Technicians. We are grateful for their permission to include this material in full.

We are grateful to HM Revenue and Customs for the provision of tax forms, which are Crown Copyright and are reproduced here with kind permission from the Office of Public Sector Information.

Information reproduced from the VAT Guide 700 is also subject to Crown Copyright.

CONTENTS

STUDY TEXT

KAPLAN PUBLISHING

INTRODUCTION

HOW TO USE THESE MATERIALS

These Kaplan Publishing learning materials have been carefully designed to make your learning experience as easy as possible and to give you the best chance of success in your AAT assessments.

They contain a number of features to help you in the study process.

The sections on the Unit Guide, the Assessment and Study Skills should be read before you commence your studies.

They are designed to familiarise you with the nature and content of the assessment and to give you tips on how best to approach your studies.

STUDY TEXT

This study text has been specially prepared for the AAT qualification.

It is written in a practical and interactive style:

- key terms and concepts are clearly defined

- all topics are illustrated with practical examples with clearly worked solutions based on sample tasks provided by the AAT in the new examining style

- frequent activities throughout the chapters ensure that what you have learnt is regularly reinforced

- 'pitfalls' and 'examination tips' help you avoid commonly made mistakes and help you focus on what is required to perform well in your assessment

- 'Test your understanding' activities are included within each chapter to apply your learning and develop your understanding.

ICONS

The study chapters include the following icons throughout.

They are designed to assist you in your studies by identifying key definitions and the points at which you can test yourself on the knowledge gained.

 Definition

These sections explain important areas of Knowledge which must be understood and reproduced in an assessment.

 Example

The illustrative examples can be used to help develop an understanding of topics before attempting the activity exercises.

 Test your understanding

These are exercises which give the opportunity to assess your understanding of all the assessment areas.

 Reference material

These boxes will direct you to the AAT reference material that you can access during your real assessment. A copy of this reference material is included as an Appendix to this document.

Quality and accuracy are of the utmost importance to us so if you spot an error in any of our products, please send an email to mykaplanreporting@kaplan.com with full details. Our Quality Co-ordinator will work with our technical team to verify the error and take action to ensure it is corrected in future editions.

UNIT GUIDE

Introduction

This Advanced level unit is about indirect tax: specifically, the tax that is referred to in the UK and throughout this unit as value added tax (VAT). The unit is designed to develop students' skills in preparing and submitting returns to the relevant tax authority in situations where the transactions that have to be included are relatively routine. However, some non-routine issues are also included in this unit.

This unit provides students with the knowledge and skills that they need to keep their employers and clients compliant with the laws and practices that apply to the indirect taxation of sales and purchases. The content is designed to ensure that students can perform these tasks relatively unsupervised, particularly in terms of routine and some non-routine VAT tasks. However, it is expected that the student will still require some management for more involved and intensive VAT transactions. It is important that the student understands and applies the VAT rules from an ethical point of view. All VAT work must be carried out with integrity, objectivity and a high degree of professional competence. There must be due care with regard to confidentiality about any personal data being processed and, from a business protection aspect, with the correct approach to professional behaviour.

Students will learn about VAT legislation and the importance of maintaining their technical knowledge through monitoring updates. Students must be taught how to complete VAT returns accurately and must understand the implications of failing to do so. Inaccuracy and omission, late submission of returns and late payment or non-payment of VAT need to be understood in terms of the sanctions and penalties that are available to the relevant tax authority.

In particular, students will learn how to calculate the VAT value correctly in different circumstances, verify the calculations of the submitted return and correctly use an accounting system to extract relevant data for the return.

The VAT registration and deregistration rules are important aspects of learning at this level, and this includes the need to monitor sales closely to avoid breaching regulations. The existence and basic terms of special VAT schemes are also important.

Students will learn about how to deal with errors made in previous VAT returns and how and when these errors are corrected. They will also learn about communicating VAT matters to relevant individuals and organisations, including the special rules that apply when goods and services are imported into and exported out of the UK and the European Union (EU).

Indirect Tax is a mandatory unit. It links with Advanced Bookkeeping, Final Accounts Preparation and Management Accounting: Costing as core subjects, and with Spreadsheets for Accounting and Ethics for Accountants to create the Advanced Diploma in Accounting.

Learning outcomes

On completion of this unit the learner will be able to:

- Understand and apply VAT legislation requirements
- Accurately complete VAT returns and submit them in a timely manner
- Understand the implications for the business of errors, omissions and late filing and payment
- Report VAT-related information within the organisation in accordance with regulatory and organisational requirement

Scope of content

To perform this unit effectively you will need to know and understand the following:

Chapter

1 **Understand and apply VAT legislation requirements**

1.1 **Identify and analyse relevant information on VAT** 1,3,7,8

Students need to know:

- relevant sources of VAT information needed by a business

- how to analyse information available and identify relevant items to extract

- how to communicate relevant regulatory information to others within the business

- the ethical and legal implications of failure to identify and apply information and regulations to the business.

1.2 **Explain the necessary interaction with the relevant tax authority** 1,2

Students need to know:

- the relevant tax authority for VAT

- the tax authority's powers to require businesses to comply with regulations about registration, record keeping, submissions of VAT returns and payment of VAT due

- that VAT is a tax on consumer spending, including knowing whether the tax falls on registered businesses or the end user

- how and when it is appropriate to obtain guidance from the relevant tax authority about VAT matters, particularly in respect of issues where there is doubt over the correct treatment

- the tax authority's rights in respect of inspection of records and control visits (students should understand what records can be inspected during a control visit; but no further detail of control visits is expected)

- the tax authority's rules about: what constitute VAT records; how long VAT records should be retained; how VAT records should be retained.

| 1.3 | **Describe the VAT registration, scheme choice and deregistration requirements** | 2,5 |

Students need to know:

- about registering for VAT

- the registration and deregistration thresholds for the normal VAT scheme, and how to apply them

- the circumstances in which voluntary registration may be beneficial to the business

- the deregistration threshold, and circumstances in which deregistration may be appropriate

- what is meant by the past turnover measure and the future turnover method, and how to comply with them in respect of registration

- the special VAT schemes that can be used by some registered businesses: the annual and cash accounting schemes, and the flat rate scheme for small businesses

- the thresholds and qualification criteria for the special VAT schemes

- why being in the normal VAT scheme or in one or more special VAT schemes affect the timing and frequency of filing returns and payment of VAT.

Chapter

1.4   VAT invoices, required information and deadlines   3

Students need to know:

- what the correct contents and form of a VAT invoice are, including:
    - the simplified VAT invoice rule
    - the e-invoicing requirements
    - standard-rated, zero-rated and exempt supplies

- how to determine the tax point of an invoice, both basic and actual, when the invoice is raised after the supply and also when there are: advance payments, deposits, continuous supplies and goods on sale or return

- the significance of the correct tax point for eligibility for special VAT schemes, applying the correct rate of VAT and determining the correct VAT for reporting

- the time limits for issuing VAT invoices, including understanding the 14-day and 30-day rules.

1.5   Maintain knowledge of legislation, regulation, guidance and codes of practice   1

Students need to know:

- where to find information regarding changes to VAT law and practice

- how to use information to determine relevant changes for the business that must be applied

- the deadline dates by which changes must be applied

- the importance of maintaining up-to-date and relevant VAT knowledge and the impact of this on the ability to act with professional competence.

Chapter

2   **Accurately complete VAT returns and submit them in a timely manner**

2.1   **Extract relevant data from the accounting records**   7, 8

Students need to know:

- how to identify relevant accounting records that cover the required period of each VAT return

- how to identify and extract relevant income, expenditure and VAT figures from the following ledgers and accounts: sales and sales returns, purchases and purchases returns, cash and petty cash accounts; and the VAT account

- how to determine that the figures extracted have come from an original and verified daybook or journal

- how to determine that entries in the ledgers have been made with integrity and due regard to the regulation of VAT administration.

2.2   **Calculate relevant input and output tax**   1, 3, 4, 7, 8

Students need to know:

- the difference between inputs and outputs, and between input tax and output tax

- the specific calculations needed for standard, reduced-rate, zero-rated and exempt supplies

- the place of supply rules for both goods and services within and outside the EU

- how to treat different forms of inputs and outputs when preparing a VAT return, including how to identify valid VAT documents for the purposes of input tax recovery

- how imports, acquisitions, despatches and exports are treated on a VAT return, but not any knowledge of Intrastat returns, EC Sales List or VAT Mini One Stop Shop

- the different implications of exempt supplies and of zero-rated supplies for the VAT return, and the effect on recovery of input tax

- how partial exemption works, the de minimis limit and how this affects the recovery of input tax

- rounding rules on VAT calculations, including for retailers

- rules for VAT when prompt payment discounts (PPD) are offered to customers, and how to calculate it

- how to calculate the VAT when given the net or the gross amount of the supply

- how to account for VAT on: expenditure on employee and business contact entertaining, including that of mixed groups; purchases and sales of cars and vans; deposits and advance payments for goods and services

- the VAT rules on fuel scale charges, how to apply them, and their effect on VAT payable or reclaimable

- how to apply bad debt relief, when this is available and what time limits apply.

Chapter

| 2.3 | Calculate the VAT due to, or from, the relevant tax authority | 7, 8 |

Students need to be able to:

- correctly calculate the VAT payable to or reclaimable from the relevant tax authority for a VAT period, in respect of: transactions in the current VAT period, including access to and use of sales and purchases invoices, credit notes issued and received, cash and petty cash transaction receipts; adjustments for bad debt relief, fuel scale charges, entertainment expenses, cars and vans, deposits and advance payments, and correction of errors and omissions made in previous returns

- disallow VAT that is not recoverable

- deal with pressure to allow irrecoverable VAT or other inappropriate amounts to appear on the VAT return, or to remain in the accounts.

| 2.4 | Make adjustments and declarations for any errors or omissions identified in previous VAT periods | 6, 7, 8 |

Students need to be able to:

- determine if a given previous period error or omission can be corrected by an amendment on the current VAT return

- apply the thresholds and deadlines within which previous period errors/omissions must be declared, including the timescales during which corrections can be made

- identify when a given previous period error or omission must be separately reported rather than corrected on the current VAT return

- apply the required treatment

- report a previous period error or omission that cannot be corrected on a current VAT return.

Chapter

2.5	**Complete and submit a VAT return and make any associated payment within statutory limits**	5,7,8

Students need to know:

- the statutory time limits for submitting VAT returns and making payment for both normal and special VAT schemes

- how these time limits differ depending on the payment method used

- how to complete all relevant boxes of the online return in the manner laid down by the relevant tax authority

- how to calculate the amount of VAT due to or reclaimable from the relevant tax authority as a check on the amounts calculated by the online VAT return

- why the final total on the VAT return should agree with the total on the business' VAT account

- how to identify the reasons why the given final total and the given VAT account differ

- the process for recovery of VAT that is to be reclaimed from the relevant tax authority.

3 **Understand the implications for the business of errors, omissions, and late filing and payment**

3.1	**Explain the implications for a business of failure to comply with registration requirements**	6

Students need to know:

- the powers of the tax authority to penalise a business that has failed to register for VAT

- the details of the penalty regime applicable to non-registration or late registration.

Chapter

3.2 **Explain the implications for a business of failure to comply with the requirement to submit VAT returns**   6

Students need to know:

- the consequences of late submission and non-submission of VAT returns

- how the surcharge regime applies to late submission or non-submission of VAT returns

- the powers of assessment the tax authority has in respect of failure to submit VAT returns.

3.3 **Explain the implications for a business of failure to comply with the requirement to make payment of VAT**   6

Students need to know:

- the consequences of late payment or non-payment of VAT due

- the details of the penalty regime applicable to late or non-payment of VAT due.

3.4 **Explain the implications for a business resulting from a failure to make error corrections in the proper manner or report errors where required to do so**   6

Students need to know:

- the consequences of failing to correct errors properly

- the consequences of failing to report an error when required to do so

- the operational, ethical and legal consequences of allowing VAT recovery that is by law disallowed.

4	**Report VAT-related information within the organisation in accordance with regulatory and organisational requirement**	
4.1	**Inform the appropriate person about VAT-related matters**	3, 7, 8

Students need to be able:

- identify the appropriate person to whom to report information, given different circumstances

- provide appropriate information regarding: the discovery of current and previous period errors and omissions; determining whether to correct or disclose errors and omissions; the completion of the return; penalties, surcharges and assessments; the effects of a change in VAT rate or other regulatory changes; the effect on VAT of a change in business operations

- communicate the appropriate time limits for submitting VAT returns to appropriate persons

- identify when a query about VAT is beyond current experience or expertise and so should be referred to a line manager.

4.2	**Communicate information about VAT due to or from the tax authority**	5, 7, 8

Students need to be able to:

- specify relevant information regarding amounts due to or recovery of amounts from the UK's Revenue and Customs authority (HMRC)

- communicate the effects of the special VAT schemes on payment or recovery of VAT.

Delivering this unit

Unit name	Content links	Suggested order of delivery
Advanced Bookkeeping and Final Accounts Preparation	VAT and its treatment is a key part of all the Bookkeeping units in this qualification, including the preparation of ledger accounts.	N/A

KAPLAN PUBLISHING

THE ASSESSMENT

Test specification for this unit assessment

Assessment type

Computer based assessment

Marking type

Computer marked

Duration of exam

1 hour 30 minutes

The assessment for this unit consists of 8 compulsory tasks.

The competency level for AAT assessment is 70%.

Learning outcomes		Weighting
1	Understand and apply VAT legislation requirements	30%
2	Accurately complete VAT returns and submit them in a timely manner	40%
3	Understand the implications for the business of errors, omissions and late filing and payment	20%
4	Report VAT related information within the organisation in accordance with regulatory and organisational requirements	10%
Total		100%

AAT reference material

Reference material is provided in this assessment. During your assessment you will be able to access reference material through a series of clickable links on the right of every task. These will produce pop-up windows which can be moved or closed.

The AAT reference material is available to study before the assessment, via the AAT website, and in the appendix to this study text.

STUDY SKILLS

Preparing to study

Devise a study plan

Determine which times of the week you will study.

Split these times into sessions of at least one hour for study of new material. Any shorter periods could be used for revision or practice.

Put the times you plan to study onto a study plan for the weeks from now until the assessment and set yourself targets for each period of study – in your sessions make sure you cover the whole course and the associated test your understanding questions.

If you are studying more than one unit at a time, try to vary your subjects as this can help to keep you interested and see subjects as part of wider knowledge.

When working through your course, compare your progress with your plan and, if necessary, re-plan your work (perhaps including extra sessions) or, if you are ahead, do some extra revision/practice questions.

Effective studying

Active reading

You are not expected to learn the text by rote, rather, you must understand what you are reading and be able to use it to pass the assessment and develop good practice.

A good technique is to use SQ3Rs – Survey, Question, Read, Recall, Review:

1   **Survey the chapter**

    Look at the headings and read the introduction, knowledge, skills and content, so as to get an overview of what the chapter deals with.

2   **Question**

    Whilst undertaking the survey ask yourself the questions you hope the chapter will answer for you.

3   Read

Read through the chapter thoroughly working through the Test your understanding questions and, at the end, making sure that you can meet the learning objectives highlighted on the first page.

4   Recall

At the end of each section and at the end of the chapter, try to recall the main ideas of the section/chapter without referring to the text. This is best done after short break of a couple of minutes after the reading stage.

5   Review

Check that your recall notes are correct.

You may also find it helpful to re-read the chapter to try and see the topic(s) it deals with as a whole.

Note taking

Taking notes is a useful way of learning, but do not simply copy out the text.

The notes must:

- be in your own words
- be concise
- cover the key points
- be well organised
- be modified as you study further chapters in this text or in related ones.

Trying to summarise a chapter without referring to the text can be a useful way of determining which areas you know and which you don't.

Three ways of taking notes

1   Summarise the key points of a chapter

2   Make linear notes

A list of headings, subdivided with sub-headings listing the key points.

If you use linear notes, you can use different colours to highlight key points and keep topic areas together.

Use plenty of space to make your notes easy to use.

3   Try a diagrammatic form

The most common of which is a mind map.

To make a mind map, put the main heading in the centre of the paper and put a circle around it.

Draw lines radiating from this to the main sub-headings which again have circles around them.

Continue the process from the sub-headings to sub-sub-headings.

Annotating the text

You may find it useful to underline or highlight key points in your study text – but do be selective.

You may also wish to make notes in the margins.

Revision phase

Kaplan has produced material specifically designed for your final examination preparation for this unit.

These include pocket revision notes and an exam kit that includes a bank of revision questions specifically in the style of the new syllabus.

Further guidance on how to approach the final stage of your studies is given in these materials.

Further reading

In addition to this text, you should also read the "Accounting Technician" magazine every month to keep abreast of any guidance from the AAT and chief assessors.

VAT REFERENCE INFORMATION

Note: This information is provided for use in this Study text.
You do **not** need to memorise this information.
It is all included in the AAT reference material.

Standard rate of VAT	20%
VAT fraction (standard-rated) (often simplified to 1/6)	20/120
Reduced rate of VAT	5%
VAT fraction (reduced-rated) (often simplifies to 1/21)	5/105
Annual registration threshold	£85,000
De-registration threshold	£83,000
Cash accounting:	
Taxable turnover threshold (excluding VAT) to join scheme	£1,350,000
Taxable turnover threshold (excluding VAT) to leave scheme	£1,600,000
Annual accounting:	
Taxable turnover threshold (excluding VAT) to join scheme	£1,350,000
Taxable turnover threshold (excluding VAT) to leave scheme	£1,600,000
Flat rate scheme:	
Taxable turnover threshold (excluding VAT) to join scheme	£150,000
Total turnover threshold (including VAT) to leave scheme	£230,000

Additional information

In your assessment you are provided with the AAT reference material.

This can be accessed by clicking the appropriate heading on the right hand side of the screen.

A copy of this AAT reference material is included in the Appendix to this textbook.

It is also available to download from the AAT website www.aat.org.uk.

It is very important that you become familiar with the content of each section of the material before you sit your assessment.

Within this text we make reference to areas of the AAT reference material which are particularly useful.

Introduction to VAT

1

Introduction

This chapter introduces some of the basic ideas of value added tax (VAT), which is the only tax studied in this paper on indirect tax.

This unit requires you to have knowledge of VAT rules, to be able to prepare VAT returns, understand VAT penalties and correction of errors, and be able to communicate VAT issues to the relevant people within an organisation.

ASSESSMENT CRITERIA
Identify and analyse relevant information on VAT (1.1)
Explain the necessary interaction with the relevant tax authority (1.2)
Maintain knowledge of legislation, regulation, guidance and codes of practice (1.5)
Calculate relevant input and output tax (2.2)

CONTENTS

1 Introduction
2 Types of supply
3 Sources of information
4 Keeping up-to-date with VAT
5 HM Revenue and Customs

1 Introduction

1.1 What is VAT?

VAT is:

- an indirect tax on consumer spending

- charged on most goods and services supplied within the UK

- suffered by the final consumer, and

- collected by businesses on behalf of HM Revenue and Customs (HMRC).

Overview of how VAT works

VAT is collected by businesses at each stage in the production and distribution process of supplying goods and services as follows:

- businesses account to HMRC for the tax (known as output VAT) on sales

- if the customer is VAT-registered and uses the goods or services for business purposes, they can recover the tax they have paid on the purchase of the item or service (known as input VAT)

- accordingly, businesses actually account to HMRC for the tax on the 'value added' to the product at that stage of the process.

Businesses are merely acting as collectors of VAT on behalf of HMRC and they do not suffer any tax.

It is only the final consumer who cannot recover the input VAT that suffers the tax.

VAT is therefore an indirect tax:

- because it is paid indirectly to traders when you buy most goods and services, rather than being collected directly by HMRC from the taxpayer as a proportion of their income or gains.

How VAT works is shown in the illustration below.

Assume that the rate of VAT throughout is 20%.

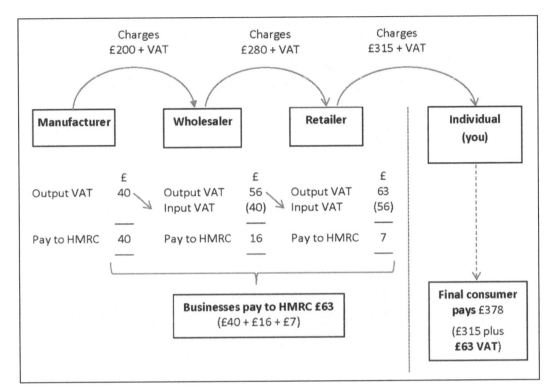

Who charges VAT?

VAT is only charged

- by **taxable persons**

- when they make **taxable supplies** in the course of their business.

VAT is not generally charged on non-business transactions.

For example, you would not have to charge VAT if you simply sold some of your spare DVDs to a friend.

1.2   Taxable persons

 Definition

Taxable persons are businesses which are (or should be) registered for VAT.

VAT registration rules are dealt with in Chapter 2.

A person can be an individual or a legal person such as a company.

1.3   Taxable supplies

Taxable supplies, or outputs, are mainly sales made by a taxable person.

Taxable supplies can also include gifts, and goods taken from the business for personal use.

1.4 Output tax

 Definition

The VAT charged on sales or taxable supplies is called **output tax**.

Taxable persons charge output tax to their customers and periodically, (usually quarterly), they pay it over to HMRC.

1.5 Input tax

When a business buys goods from or pays expenses (inputs) to a VAT-registered supplier, then it will also be paying VAT on those purchases or expenses.

 Definition

VAT paid by a business on purchases or expenses is called **input tax**.

VAT-registered businesses are allowed to reclaim their input tax.

They do this by deducting the input tax they have paid from the output tax which they owe, and paying over the net amount only.

If the input tax exceeds the output tax, then the balance is recoverable from HMRC.

 Example

A VAT-registered business makes sales of £10,000 plus £2,000 of VAT. Its expenditure on purchases and expenses totals £7,000 plus £1,400 of VAT.

How much VAT is payable to HMRC?

Solution

	£
Output VAT	2,000.00
Less: Input VAT	(1,400.00)
VAT due	600.00

This means that registered businesses do not suffer VAT themselves. It is the end consumer of the goods (e.g. a member of the public like you) who suffers the VAT, as they cannot recover the VAT they have been charged.

Test your understanding 1

Which of the following is the correct definition of a taxable person?

A   A business which is registered for VAT

B   A business which should be registered for VAT

C   A business which is or should be registered for VAT

D   A business which makes standard-rated supplies

 Test your understanding 2

Indicate whether the following statements are true or false.

Tick one box on each line.

		True	False
1	VAT is a direct tax.		
2	Jake is an AAT student working for a small accountancy practice. He advertises his bicycle for sale on the work notice board and sells the bicycle to one of his workmates for £100. He should not charge VAT on the sale.		
3	Businesses may keep all the VAT they collect from customers.		
4	Fred runs a small plumbing business which is registered for VAT. He replaces a tap for a customer and charges them £60 including VAT of £10. The VAT charge of £10 is retained by Fred.		

2 Types of supply

2.1 Classification of supplies

Supplies can be **taxable**, **exempt** or **outside the scope** of VAT.

VAT is charged on taxable supplies but **not on exempt supplies** or supplies outside the scope of VAT. It is therefore important to be able to correctly classify supplies in order to determine whether VAT should be charged.

Exempt supplies are supplies that the law states should not have VAT charged on them, such as insurance. Specific knowledge of which supplies are exempt will not be tested in your assessment.

Supplies outside the scope of VAT include items such as wages and dividends. They are ignored for VAT purposes.

2.2 Taxable supplies – rates of VAT

Taxable supplies are charged to VAT at one of three rates:

- **Zero rate**: This is a tax rate of nil. No output VAT is charged but it is classed as a taxable supply. Therefore it is taken into account in deciding whether a trader should register for VAT and whether input VAT is recoverable.

- **Reduced rate**: Some supplies, mainly for domestic and charitable purposes are charged at the reduced rate.

- **Standard rate**: Any taxable supply which is not charged at the zero or reduced rates is charged at the standard rate.

Currently **the standard** rate of VAT is 20% and the reduced rate is 5%.

In order to calculate the VAT on a **VAT-exclusive** supply which is taxable at the standard rate, you multiply by 20%.

If taxable at the reduced rate, you multiply by 5%.

In order to calculate the VAT on a **VAT-inclusive** supply which is taxable at the standard rate, you multiply by 20/120). This is sometimes simplified to 1/6.

If the VAT-inclusive supply is taxable at the reduced rate then you multiply by 5/105. This is sometimes simplified to 1/21.

These rates are summarised in the following table:

Rate of VAT	% to apply to VAT-exclusive amounts to calculate VAT	Fraction to apply to VAT-inclusive amounts to calculate VAT
Standard	20%	20/120 or 1/6
Reduced	5%	5/105 or 1/21

 Example

A business makes the following taxable sales.

What is the output VAT in each case (to the nearest pence)?

(i) a standard-rated supply which is £12,000 net of VAT
(£12,000 × 20%) = £2,400.00

(ii) £12,000 inclusive of the standard rate of VAT
(£12,000 × 20/120) = £2,000.00

(iii) £15,479 net of reduced rate VAT
(£15,479 × 5%) = £773.95

(iv) £12,320 inclusive of reduced rate VAT
(£12,320 × 5/105) = £586.67

Note that VAT on an invoice is rounded down to the nearest pence (Chapter 3).

 Test your understanding 3

Calculate the amount of VAT in respect of the following amounts.

Calculate to the nearest pence.

Item	Rate of VAT	VAT-inclusive amount £	VAT-exclusive amount £	VAT £ p
1	20%	472.50		
2	20%		5,250.00	
3	5%		4,230.00	
4	5%	4,284.00		

2.3 Effect of making taxable supplies

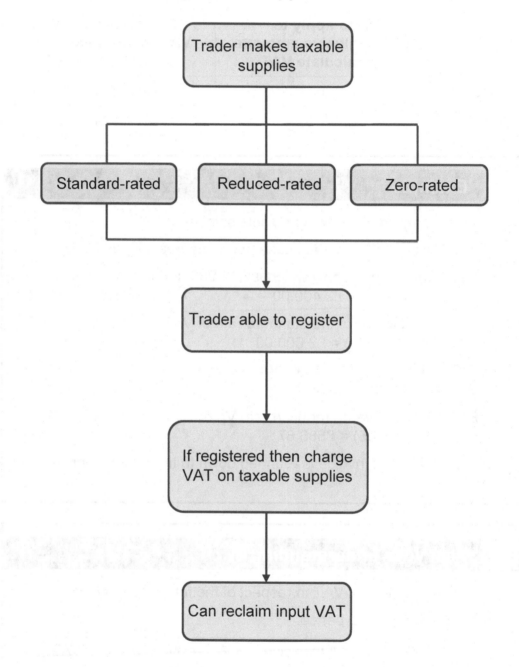

2.4 Differences between zero-rated and exempt supplies

You must be careful to distinguish between traders making zero-rated supplies and those making exempt supplies.

	Exempt	Zero-rated
Can register for VAT?	No	Yes
Charge output VAT to customers?	No	Yes at 0%
Can recover input tax?	No	Yes

 Test your understanding 4

Select which word(s) in italics complete(s) the following sentences correctly.

1 Traders making only exempt supplies …*can/must/cannot*…… register for VAT.

2 Traders who are registered for VAT must charge VAT on all of their ….*taxable/exempt*… supplies.

3 One of the differences between traders making zero-rated supplies and traders making exempt supplies is that zero-rated traders …….*can/cannot*… recover input VAT, whereas exempt traders …..*can/cannot*.

2.5 Examples of zero-rated and exempt supplies

You do not need to learn lists of zero-rated and exempt items. These examples are simply to show you the types of items in each category.

Zero-rated	Exempt
Water	Rent
Most food	Insurance
Books and newspapers	Postal services
Public transport	Finance (e.g. making loans)
Children's clothes and shoes	Education (not for profit)
New house building	Betting and lotteries

Test your understanding 5

Indicate whether the following statements are true or false.
Tick one box on each line.

		True	*False*
1	Output tax must be charged on all sales made by a registered trader.		
2	VAT is borne by the final consumer.		
3	Registered traders making zero-rated supplies cannot recover any input tax.		

 Reference material

Some information about the scope of VAT, taxable and exempt supplies is included in the indirect tax reference material provided in the real assessment, so you do not need to learn it.

It can be found in the 'Introduction', 'Rates of VAT' and 'Exempt and partly-exempt businesses' sections.

You need to be familiar with the location and content of the material as in the assessment you will need to access the correct part of the reference material from a series of clickable links.

Why not look up the correct part of the indirect tax reference material in the appendix to this text book now?

3 Sources of information

3.1 Legislation

The main source of law on VAT is the VAT Act 1994 as amended by annual Finance Acts and other regulations issued by Parliament.

3.2 GOV.UK website

HMRC expect taxpayers to be able to answer many of their queries by searching the HMRC section of the gov.uk website at:

https://www.gov.uk/topic/business-tax/vat

HMRC publications can be searched online. Some sections are available as pdfs and can be downloaded.

Publications available include:

- VAT guide 700 (see below)

- VAT Notes (see below)

- information sheets on particular topics.

HMRC also provide educational and explanatory material online including:

- YouTube videos

- Live webinars with links to recordings of past webinars.

Businesses can also sign up to receive emails about VAT.

3.3 VAT guide

HMRC issue a booklet called the **VAT Guide** Notice 700. This is the main guide to VAT rules and procedures. There are a number of supplements and amendments to the Guide to keep it up-to-date.

The VAT Guide is also available online on the HMRC section of the gov.uk website. As it is a large document (over 250 pages long) it is broken into sections on the website. It can be searched online or downloaded.

If you are dealing with accounting for VAT and VAT returns in practice, then you should become familiar with the contents of the VAT Guide in order to be able to refer to it when necessary.

 Example

If you wish to look up more information about the topics covered so far in this chapter, then Section 3 of the VAT guide has the following:

3 General explanation of VAT: introduction and liability

    3.1 Introduction to VAT

    3.2 What is VAT?

    3.3 VAT rates

    3.4 Reduced-rated supplies

    3.5 Zero-rated supplies

    3.6 Exempt supplies

    3.7 Further information on liability and rates of VAT

3.4 VAT Notes

HMRC also publish a quarterly bulletin called VAT Notes. This is sent to all registered traders and contains a summary of all recent changes to the VAT rules and announces future changes. It is also available online.

3.5 VAT enquiries helpline

If a taxpayer cannot find the answer to their queries on the HMRC website then a telephone helpline is available. When you call you should have a note of your VAT registration number and postcode.

Taxpayers can also email or write to HMRC with VAT queries.

 Reference material

Some information about HMRC website and the VAT enquiries helpline is included in the indirect tax reference material provided in the real assessment, so you do not need to learn it.

It can be found in the 'Finding out more information about VAT' section.

You need to be familiar with the location and content of the material as in the assessment you will need to access the correct part of the reference material from a series of clickable links.

Why not look up the correct part of indirect tax reference material in the appendix to this text book now?

 Keeping up-to-date with VAT

4.1 Introduction

VAT changes regularly as a result of new legislation, VAT case decisions and changes in EU rules.

It is important for everyone involved in VAT work to keep up-to-date, as failing to apply VAT rules correctly can cost the business money and may lead to penalties for incorrect returns or underpayments.

From an ethical point of view, it is important for AAT members and students to keep up-to-date in order that they may give competent advice.

Changes in VAT regulations normally take effect on a specified date and a business must ensure that they comply with the new rules from that date.

4.2 Continuing professional development (CPD)

The AAT expects all full and fellow members to undertake continuing professional development (CPD) each year to ensure they are up-to-date and competent to do their work.

For a member involved in VAT work this would include being aware of any new rules and regulations.

4.3 Ways of keeping up-to-date

Information about VAT changes is circulated by HMRC in their quarterly VAT notes mentioned above.

Other sources of information about changes would include:

- the UK government website which has a VAT section (see above)
- circulars from accountancy firms – most firms issue a newsletter to clients which can often be accessed on their website
- specialist tax journals
- CPD courses
- networking meetings with fellow professionals.

4.4 Ethical considerations

AAT members and students are required to follow the AAT Code of Professional Ethics. These require that AAT members act with:

- integrity
- objectivity
- professional competence and due care
- confidentiality
- professional behaviour.

It is important to keep up-to-date with VAT legislation and any changes in order to act with professional competence and due care.

4.5 Impact on an organisation's recording systems

Legislative changes can have a significant impact on the recording systems of both HMRC and businesses with associated costs to be incurred to reflect the changes.

For example, when the rates of VAT change, supplies are reclassified, registration thresholds and/or registration rules change, significant costs can arise for a business.

Additional costs may include:

- staff training (and/or recruitment)

- adapting IT systems

- purchasing new software

- reprinting stationery, and

- additional time required for administrative (non-productive) work as opposed to profit-generating work.

More details on the impact of VAT rate changes on a business can be found in Chapter 3.

5 HM Revenue and Customs

5.1 Introduction

As mentioned above, **HM Revenue and Customs** (HMRC) is the government body that is responsible for administering VAT.

VAT offices across the country are responsible for the local administration of VAT within a particular geographical area.

Local VAT offices deal with the collection of outstanding tax and carry out visits to taxpayers to check that they are complying with VAT rules.

HMRC are also responsible for dealing with all other issues concerning VAT including registration and record keeping (see below for record keeping requirements).

5.2 HMRC powers

HMRC have certain powers that help it administer VAT. These include:

- inspecting premises

- examining records

- making assessments for underpaid tax

- charging penalties for breaches of VAT rules (more detail on penalties can be found in Chapter 6)

- determining whether certain supplies are liable for VAT.

5.3 Visits by VAT officers

VAT officers can visit premises to inspect records and make checks.

(see Chapter 2 for more details on VAT records).

🗒️ Reference material

More information about visits by VAT officers is included in the indirect tax reference material provided in the real assessment, so you do not need to learn it.

It can be found in the 'Visits by VAT officers' section.

You need to be familiar with the location and content of the material as in the assessment you will need to access the correct part of the reference material from a series of clickable links.

Why not look up the correct part of the indirect tax reference material in the appendix to this text book now?

5.4 HMRC rulings

HMRC will give rulings on how they will deal with particular transactions.

Obtaining a ruling on areas of difficulty is recommended by HMRC.

You may need to write to HMRC in the following cases:

- you've looked at all the published information and can't find the answer to your question

- HMRC published guidance is unclear when applied to your particular situation

- you've already contacted the helpline and they've asked you to write.

An HMRC ruling is binding on HMRC provided the taxpayer has disclosed all the necessary facts.

However, it is not binding on the taxpayer who may choose to ignore the ruling.

Ignoring the ruling will almost certainly lead to a dispute with HMRC that will need to be resolved by the Tax Tribunal.

5.5 Communicating with HMRC

Note that in practice, HMRC expect taxpayers to adhere to the following sequence when they have a query about VAT:

- check the information publicly available in the VAT Guide 700, on their website; and then

- raise the matter with the helpline

- before submitting a query.

If the query turns out to be something on which HMRC already publish information, they will reply explaining where the information can be found.

 Reference material

More information about communicating with HMRC is included in the indirect tax reference material provided in the real assessment, so you do not need to learn it.

It can be found in the 'Finding out more information about VAT' section.

You need to be familiar with the location and content of the material as in the assessment you will need to access the correct part of the reference material from a series of clickable links.

Why not look up the correct part of the indirect tax reference material in the appendix to this text book now?

5.6 Disputes with HMRC

Most disagreements between the taxpayer and HMRC are resolved quickly, but if an agreement cannot be reached then the taxpayer has a choice of actions.

(1)   Ask for their case to be reviewed by another HMRC officer who has not previously been involved with the matter.

(2)   If they do not wish the case to be reviewed by another officer, or if they disagree with the review findings, the taxpayer can appeal to the Tax Tribunal. Such appeals are made initially to the First-tier Tax Tribunal. If the matter cannot be resolved there it may be appealed upwards to the Upper Tribunal and from there to the Court of Appeal and then the Supreme Court.

The ultimate legal authority on VAT matters is the European Court of Justice.

6 Test your understanding

Test your understanding 6

Which one of the following is NOT a power of HMRC?

A   Inspecting premises

B   Completing your VAT return

C   Examining records

D   Determining whether certain supplies are liable for VAT

Test your understanding 7

Which of the following is **NOT** a good source of information on VAT?

A   The HMRC website

B   A taxation magazine with a VAT section

C   VAT Notes

D   A CPD course on direct taxation

Test your understanding 8

Which one of the following is **NOT** a good reason to keep up-to-date with VAT?

A   It enables you to act with competence

B   Keeping up-to-date means that you are able to advise the business you work for and make it less likely to incur a penalty for a breach of the VAT rules

C   If you are up-to-date with the rules then it is easier to find ways around them and avoid paying over the VAT you have charged to customers

D   It may save the business money if it applies the rules correctly

7 Summary

In this introductory chapter we have looked at some of the basic principles and terminology used when dealing with VAT.

You should now understand that VAT is an indirect tax borne by the final consumer but collected on behalf of the government by businesses.

An important area covered in this chapter is the distinction between taxable and exempt supplies. Businesses making only exempt supplies cannot register for VAT or reclaim input tax.

If you need to find out more about VAT then it is important to know where to look. The VAT guide 700 and the HMRC website cover everything a typical business would need to know about VAT. Of course, you do not need to know all this material; you simply need to know where you might look to find it.

It is important from a professional competence point of view to keep up-to-date on VAT and there are a number of ways in which you can find out the latest information about VAT.

It is also important to appreciate the cost implications of implementing new legislation and the significance and potential costs of mistakes made as a result of not being up-to-date.

Communicating with HMRC is an important issue in practice. You must understand the importance of obtaining rulings on contentious matters in writing.

Test your understanding answers

Test your understanding 1

The correct answer is C.

Test your understanding 2

1   False – VAT is an indirect tax.

2   True – VAT is charged on business transactions so the statement is correct. Jake does not need to charge VAT on the sale of his bicycle.

3   False – Businesses collect VAT on behalf of the government so this statement is incorrect.

4   False – As Fred's business is registered for VAT he must account to HMRC for any output VAT charged to his customers.

Test your understanding 3

1   £78.75 (£472.50 × 20/120)

2   £1,050.00 (£5,250 × 20%)

3   £211.50 (£4,230 × 5%)

4   £204.00 (£4,284 × 5/105)

Test your understanding 4

1   Cannot

2   Taxable

3   Can
    Cannot

Test your understanding 5

1   False – some sales may be exempt

2   True

3   False – zero-rated supplies are taxable supplies so VAT can be recovered

 Test your understanding 6

The correct answer is B.

A, C and D are all powers of HMRC.

 Test your understanding 7

The correct answer is D.

VAT is an indirect tax so a CPD course on direct taxation would not be a good source of information on VAT.

The other three options are all ways of finding information about VAT.

 Test your understanding 8

The correct answer is C.

AAT members and students are required to act with professional competence.

Avoiding paying VAT due to HMRC is in breach of professional competence and will lead to penalties (and possible criminal charges).

VAT registration

Introduction

This chapter introduces the rules for both compulsory and voluntary VAT registration. It also explains when a business must deregister.

If a business does not register for VAT when it starts then a careful eye must be kept on the level of taxable turnover (standard, reduced and zero-rated supplies), to avoid missing the deadline for registration.

Remember from Chapter 1 that a taxable person is one who is, or should be, registered for VAT. This means that even if a trader does not register, they may still have a liability for VAT and they may be charged a penalty.

It is important for a business to keep the correct records both for their business and for VAT purposes. This is dealt with in this chapter.

ASSESSMENT CRITERIA	CONTENTS
Explain the necessary interaction with the relevant tax authority (1.2)	1 Compulsory registration
	2 Consequences of registration
Describe the VAT registration, scheme choice and deregistration requirements (1.3)	3 Voluntary registration
	4 Deregistration
	5 Record keeping

1 Compulsory registration

1.1 Introduction

Not all businesses need to register for VAT even if they make taxable supplies. It is only businesses that have taxable supplies exceeding the registration threshold that have to register under the compulsory registration rules.

There are two separate tests for compulsory registration:

- Historic test

- Future prospects test.

1.2 Turnover for registration purposes

Turnover for VAT registration purposes comprises of taxable supplies.

Taxable supplies for this purpose:

- includes all taxable supplies (standard, reduced and zero-rated), but

- excludes output VAT, and

- excludes sales of capital assets.

Exempt supplies are not included in turnover for the purposes of deciding whether a business should register for VAT.

1.3 Historic test

At the end of each month, the trader must look at the cumulative total of taxable supplies for the last 12 months (or since starting in business if this is less than 12 months ago).

If the total exceeds the registration threshold of £85,000 the trader must register as follows.

- Notify HMRC **within 30 days** of the end of the month in which the turnover threshold is exceeded.

  Notification can be made either online or by post.

- Registration is effective from the **first day of the second month** after the turnover exceeded the threshold, or an agreed earlier date.

- A trader need not register if his taxable supplies for the next 12 months are expected to be less than the deregistration threshold of £83,000 (see below).

  This helps businesses whose annual turnover is usually below the registration threshold but have experienced one particularly good year.

Reference material

Information about registration thresholds is included in the indirect tax reference material provided in the real assessment, so you do not need to learn it.

It can be found in the 'Registration and deregistration' section.

You need to be familiar with the location and content of the material as in the assessment you will need to access the correct part of the reference material from a series of clickable links.

Why not look up the correct part of the indirect tax reference material in the appendix to this text book now?

 Example

Tariq started in business on 1 January 20X0. His taxable turnover is £10,000 per month.

He checks his taxable turnover at the end of each month and discovers at the end of September 20X0 that his taxable supplies for the previous 9 months have exceeded the registration threshold.

He must notify HMRC by 30 October and will be registered with effect from 1 November or an agreed earlier date.

 Test your understanding 1

Deanna starts a business on 1 June 20X0.

Her monthly turnover of taxable supplies is £8,600.

1   Assuming the registration threshold is £85,000, when does Deanna have to notify HMRC of her liability to register and from which date would she normally be registered?

2   Would your answer to (1) be any different if Deanna's turnover was made up of half standard-rated and half zero-rated supplies?

3   Would your answer to (1) be any different if Deanna's turnover was made up wholly of exempt supplies?

1.4 Future prospects test

A liability to register will also arise if taxable supplies within the next 30 days are expected to exceed the registration threshold of £85,000.

This test is applied at any time, not just the end of a month, and only looks at the supplies to be made from that date in the next 30 days in isolation.

- HMRC must be notified **before the end** of the 30 day period.
- Registration will be effective from the **beginning** of the 30 day period.

 Example

Dog Ltd signs a lease for new business premises on 1 June 20X0 and opens for business on 15 September 20X0. The company estimates that taxable supplies will be £90,000 per month starting immediately.

Assuming the registration threshold is £85,000, when does Dog Ltd have to register for VAT and notify HMRC?

Solution

Dog Ltd is liable to register for VAT because taxable supplies for the 30 days to 14 October 20X0 are expected to exceed £85,000.

The company must notify HMRC of its liability to register by 14 October 20X0 and is registered with effect from 15 September 20X0.

Note: Dog Ltd does not make any taxable supplies before September 20X0 so does not need to register before that date.

 Test your understanding 2

State which of the following unregistered traders are liable to register for VAT and the effective date of registration.

Name	Supplies	Details
Majid	Accountancy services (standard-rated)	Started in business on 1 October 20X0. Estimated fees of £18,000 per month.
Jane	Baby wear (zero-rated)	Established the business on 1 July 20X0 when Jane signed a contract to supply a local nursery. Sales for July 20X0 are expected to be £100,000.

Sayso Ltd	Insurance broker (exempt)	Commenced trading 2 August 20X0 with expected sales of £100,000 per month.
Omar	Stationers (standard-rated)	Has traded for many years with a normal turnover of around £60,000. A one-off successful month in July 20X5 made total sales for the 12 m/e 31 December 20X5 £86,000. Sales have since reverted to normal levels and are expected to continue at the same level.

 Test your understanding 3

You are given the following information about the taxable supplies of four businesses.

Assuming that the registration threshold is £85,000, for each of the businesses select whether they need to register for VAT immediately, or monitor turnover and register later.

Tick one box on each line.

		Register now	Monitor and register later
1	A new business with an expected taxable turnover of £87,000 per month for the next 12 months.		
2	An existing business with a total taxable turnover of £75,200 since it began trading 11 months ago. The taxable turnover for the next month is not known.		
3	An existing business with a taxable turnover of £7,190 per month for the last 12 months.		
4	An existing business with a taxable turnover of £6,000 per month since it began trading six months ago which is expected to increase to £9,000 per month for the next six months.		

Test your understanding 4

Brown commenced in business on 1 February 20X1 making only taxable supplies. His turnover was as follows:

First 6 months to 31.7.20X1   £5,000 per month

Next 12 months to 31.7.20X2   £7,800 per month

1   On which of the following dates does Brown exceed the registration threshold of £85,000?

      A   31 January 20X2

      B   28 February 20X2

      C   31 March 20X2

      D   30 April 20X2

2   Select the date by which Brown should notify HMRC that he has exceeded the registration threshold.

      A   2 March 20X2

      B   30 March 20X2

      C   30 April 20X2

      D   30 May 20X2

1.5   Number of registrations

A 'person' is registered for VAT. A 'person' is an individual, partnership or company.

An individual sole trader has only one registration, and this registration includes all the sole trader businesses that the individual carries on.

Where a partnership is concerned, a separate registration is required for the partnership. Other unincorporated businesses carried on by the individual partners will have separate registration (as explained above).

Companies are all registered individually although it is possible for companies in certain sorts of groups to have a group registration. You do not need to know any details of this.

If one company takes over another company then they both continue with their individual registrations, unless they opt for a group registration.

If an unincorporated business is sold to a company, then the registration of the unincorporated business will cease, unless the company is not yet registered in which case it may be possible to transfer the registration across.

Example

Jason is a sole trader. He owns a clothing shop "Jason's Style" which is open during the day. In the evenings he runs a business organising parties. Both businesses have a turnover of £45,000.

Jason is also a partner in Bash and Co, an import/export business he helps run with his wife. The partnership business has a turnover of £100,000.

Assuming the entire turnover of all of the businesses consists of taxable supplies, how many VAT registrations are required?

Solution

There are two registrations needed here:

(a)   One registration is needed to cover Jason's two sole trader businesses.

Even though each business has taxable turnover below the registration threshold, the combined taxable turnover of the businesses is over the threshold.

(b)   One registration will cover Bash and Co, the partnership.

 Test your understanding 5

Wayne runs three sole trader businesses and is also in partnership with his wife running a fourth business.

Each of the businesses has taxable supplies exceeding the VAT registration threshold.

How many VAT registrations are required?

A   1

B   2

C   3

D   4

1.6 Exemption from registration

A trader making **only** zero-rated supplies can apply for exemption from registration.

However, this would mean they cannot recover their input tax, and so the exemption is only likely to be applied for if:

- the trader does not want the administrative burden of complying with VAT regulations, or

- they do not have much input tax to recover.

2 Consequences of registration

2.1 Accounting for VAT

Once registered, a taxable person must start accounting for VAT.

- Output tax must be charged on taxable supplies.

- Each registered trader is allocated a VAT registration number, which must be quoted on all invoices.

- Each registered trader is allocated a tax period for filing returns, which is normally every three months and usually fits in with their accounting year end.

- Input tax on most business purchases and expenses can be recovered. This can also include certain input VAT incurred before registration. Some exceptions are dealt with in Chapter 4.

- Appropriate VAT records must be kept (see section 5 below).

Traders will be sent a certificate of registration which contains their registration number and is their proof of registration.

2.2 Changes to registration details

Certain changes to business details must be notified to HMRC within 30 days of the relevant change, otherwise a penalty may be charged.

Notifiable changes include changes to:

- business address

- bank account details

- business name

- main business activities (especially if the business will be changing the type of supply it makes).

2.3 Failure to register

A trader might think they could avoid VAT by not registering. However, if a trader does not register when they go over the compulsory registration threshold then there are two consequences.

(i)   All the VAT that the trader **should have charged** from the date they **should have registered** is payable to HMRC.

(ii)   A penalty can be charged, which is a percentage of the VAT due. Penalties are dealt with in Chapter 6.

Traders have a choice when calculating the VAT they should have charged. They can either:

(i)   treat their sales as VAT-inclusive and suffer the cost of the VAT themselves, or

(ii)   add VAT to the invoice costs and try to recover this from their customers.

Option (ii) is unlikely as customers are under no obligation to pay this VAT. This means that the business which has failed to register on time will have to pay the VAT to HMRC out of their own profits.

This illustrates how important it is to keep up-to-date and monitor turnover.

 Example

Beverley runs a business manufacturing silicon cookware which is a standard-rated supply. She has failed to register for VAT.

On 1 October 20X0 she discovers she should have been registered since 1 March 20X0. Her turnover since that date is £27,000.

The invoices will normally be treated as VAT-inclusive, so she will have to pay VAT to HMRC of £4,500 (20/120 × £27,000) less any input tax she has suffered in this period.

This VAT will be a cost to the business.

> ### Reference material
>
> Information about changes to registration details and failure to register is included in the indirect tax reference material provided in the real assessment, so you do not need to learn it.
>
> It can be found in the 'Registration and deregistration' section.
>
> You need to be familiar with the location and content of the material as in the assessment you will need to access the correct part of the reference material from a series of clickable links.
>
> Why not look up the correct part of the indirect tax reference material in the appendix to this text book now?

3 Voluntary registration

3.1 Actual or intending traders

Even if they are not required to register, a person can register provided they are **making or intending to make taxable supplies**.

HMRC will register the trader from the date of the request for voluntary registration, or a mutually agreed earlier date.

Remember that a trader who only makes exempt supplies cannot register.

3.2 Advantages and disadvantages of voluntary registration

Advantages	Disadvantages
Avoids penalties for late registration.	Business will have to comply with the VAT administration rules which may take time away from running the business.
Can recover input VAT on purchases and expenses.	Business must charge VAT. This makes their goods more expensive than an unregistered trader selling the same items or services. This extra cost cannot be recovered by unregistered customers such as the general public.
Can disguise the small size of the business.	

Test your understanding 6

Which one of the following is a valid reason for a business making taxable supplies to choose to register voluntarily?

A   Preparation of VAT returns would be optional

B   The business would be able to reclaim input VAT

C   It would make their prices cheaper to the general public

D   It would make their prices cheaper to VAT-registered customers

4 Deregistration

4.1 Compulsory deregistration

A person **must** deregister when he ceases to make taxable supplies.

- HMRC should be notified within 30 days of ceasing to make taxable supplies.

- VAT registration is cancelled from the date of cessation or a mutually agreed later date.

4.2 Voluntary deregistration

A person **may** voluntarily deregister, even if the business continues, if there is evidence that taxable supplies in the next 12 months will not exceed the deregistration threshold.

The deregistration threshold is always slightly lower than the registration threshold, and is currently £83,000.

- The 12 month period can start at any time. It does not have to be the beginning or end of a month.

- The trader must prove to HMRC that they qualify.

- VAT registration is cancelled from the date of the request or an agreed later date.

4.3 Effect of deregistration

On deregistration, VAT output tax must be paid over on the value of capital assets and inventory owned at the date of deregistration.

This takes back the input tax relief that the business would have had when it bought those assets.

Test your understanding 7

(a) Jig Ltd closed down its business on 10 October 20X0.

State when Jig Ltd should notify HMRC of the business cessation and from when the business will be deregistered.

(b) At 1 May 20X0, Eli thinks that his taxable turnover for the year to 30 April 20X1 will be below the deregistration threshold. He immediately applies for deregistration.

State when Eli will be deregistered.

 Reference material

Information about deregistration thresholds is included in the indirect tax reference material provided in the real assessment, so you do not need to learn it.

It can be found in the 'Registration and deregistration' section.

You need to be familiar with the location and content of the material as in the assessment you will need to access the correct part of the reference material from a series of clickable links.

Why not look up the correct part of the indirect tax reference material in the appendix to this text book now?

 Test your understanding 8

You are given the following information about four traders. Identify whether or not the trader **must** register for VAT.

Tick one box on each line.

		Yes	No
1	A trader making only zero-rated supplies of £100,000 per annum.		
2	A trader who has taxable supplies of £86,000 for the last 12 months, but who expects to make only £60,000 of taxable supplies in the next 12 months.		

3	An unincorporated trader who runs two separate businesses making standard-rated supplies of £50,000 each.		
4	An unincorporated trader who runs two separate businesses making annual standard-rated supplies of £65,000 in one business and annual exempt supplies of £22,000 in the other.		

5 Record keeping

5.1 General requirements

Businesses must keep information which will allow the business to calculate VAT correctly and allow HMRC to check VAT returns adequately.

Generally, the business must keep records of:

- all taxable and exempt supplies made in the course of business

- all taxable supplies received in the course of business

- the total output tax and input tax for each tax period – the VAT account (see Chapter 7).

Failure to keep records can lead to a penalty.

The business must keep records to prove the figures shown on the VAT returns for the previous **six** years, although HMRC can reduce this period where the records are bulky and the information they contain can be provided in another way.

Records may be stored electronically, particularly if this facilitates easier storage and access.

5.2 Business records

Records need to be kept for business purposes and for VAT purposes.

Business records that should be kept are:

- annual accounts including statements of profit or loss (income statements)

- bank statements, paying-in slips and cheque stubs

- cash books and other account books

- orders and delivery notes

- purchases and sales day books

- recordings of daily takings, including till rolls

- relevant business correspondence.

5.3 VAT records

VAT records are needed to allow the calculation of amounts owed to HMRC or due from HMRC in each VAT period.

Records do not have to be kept in any particular way. However it must be possible for HMRC to check the records and see how the figures in your VAT return have been calculated.

Records that should be kept include:

- records of all the standard-rated, reduced-rated, zero-rated and exempt goods and services that you buy or sell

- purchase invoices (except for purchases of £25 or less purchased through a coin operated machine, e.g. car parking) (see Chapter 3)

- copy sales invoices (see Chapter 3)

- any credit or debit notes issued or received (see Chapter 3)

- records of goods and services bought for which you cannot reclaim VAT

- import and export documents

- any adjustments or corrections to your VAT account or VAT invoices

- a VAT account.

Reference material

Information about record keeping is included in the indirect tax reference material provided in the real assessment, so you do not need to learn it.

It can be found in the 'Keeping business records and VAT records' section.

You need to be familiar with the location and content of the material as in the assessment you will need to access the correct part of the reference material from a series of clickable links.

Why not look up the correct part of the indirect tax reference material in the appendix to this text book now?

Registered businesses may be visited by a VAT officer on occasion to ensure that their records are being correctly maintained.

5.4 Electronic and paper VAT records

As long as the VAT records meet the requirements laid down by HMRC, they can be kept in whatever format the business prefers (i.e. paper and/or electronic).

Where a business keeps all or part of its records on a computer, it must make sure that the records are easily accessible if a VAT officer visits.

Records can be kept on microfilm provided HMRC have given approval and the records can be inspected when necessary.

Some businesses send or receive invoices by electronic means. This does not require approval from HMRC.

5.5 VAT account

The VAT account is an important link between the business records and the VAT return. There is no set way in which it must be kept but it must include:

- the VAT owed on sales

- the VAT that can be reclaimed on purchases and expenses

- the VAT on any EU acquisitions (purchases) or dispatches (sales) (see Chapter 8)

- error corrections

- bad debt relief.

Reference material

Information about the VAT account is included in the indirect tax reference material provided in the real assessment, so you do not need to learn it.

It can be found in the 'Keeping business records and VAT records' section.

You need to be familiar with the location and content of the material as in the assessment you will need to access the correct part of the reference material from a series of clickable links.

Why not look up the correct part of the indirect tax reference material in the appendix to this text book now?

6 Test your understanding

Test your understanding 9

Assuming that the registration threshold is £85,000, indicate whether the following statements are true or false. Tick one box on each line.

		True	False
1	An unregistered trader can never have a VAT liability to HMRC.		
2	A trader making only taxable supplies of £50,000 per annum cannot register for VAT.		
3	A trader making only exempt supplies of £100,000 per annum must register for VAT.		
4	A trader's VAT registration number must be quoted on all of their invoices.		
5	A registered trader must deregister if their taxable supplies fall below the deregistration threshold.		

Test your understanding 10

Ahmed has been in business for several years. He makes only standard-rated supplies but is not yet registered for VAT.

His monthly turnover is £6,400. On 1 June 20X3 he accepts an order with a sales value of £87,000 to be delivered at the end of June.

Which one of the following statements about Ahmed's VAT registration is correct?

A   The taxable turnover for the last 12 months is below the registration threshold so Ahmed is not yet required to register.

B   Ahmed will have to register at the end of June when his taxable turnover for the last 12 months will exceed the registration threshold.

C   Ahmed must register without delay because the new order is for an amount exceeding the VAT threshold.

7 Summary

In this chapter we have considered which traders need to become VAT-registered and the effects of registration.

Both the historic and future prospects test for registration have been set out. Remember that it is the turnover of taxable supplies, including zero-rated supplies, that determines whether a business needs to register for VAT.

It is also important to remember that businesses which **only** make **exempt** supplies **cannot** register for VAT whilst businesses that **only** make **zero-rated** supplies **need not** register for VAT if they do not wish to do so.

Failure to register when taxable supplies have exceeded the threshold can cost a business a great deal.

Firstly they must pay over the VAT they should have collected from customers and secondly they may be charged a penalty.

Traders can choose to register voluntarily provided they are making taxable supplies now or intend to in the future.

This allows the business to recover input tax, but may make the price of their goods comparatively more expensive than those of an unregistered trader.

We saw that a business **must** deregister if it ceases to make taxable supplies, and **may** deregister if its taxable supplies for the next 12 months will be below the deregistration threshold.

Finally the records that must be kept by a registered business were discussed.

Test your understanding answers

 Test your understanding 1

1 Deanna's taxable turnover will exceed £85,000 after 10 months which is at the end of March 20X1. She must notify HMRC by 30 April 20X1 and will be registered with effect from 1 May 20X1.

2 No – taxable supplies includes both standard-rated and zero-rated supplies.

3 Yes – traders who only make exempt supplies cannot register for VAT.

 Test your understanding 2

Majid will exceed the registration threshold after 5 months in business, that is, at the end of February 20X1. He must notify HMRC by 30 March and will be registered from 1 April.

Jane must register under the future prospects test as her sales will immediately exceed the registration threshold within the next 30 days. She must notify HMRC by 30 July 20X0 and will be registered from 1 July 20X0.

Sayso Ltd cannot register as it only makes exempt supplies.

Omar's taxable supplies for the 12 months ended 31 December 20X5 exceeded the threshold of £85,000. However, he does not expect his taxable supplies in the following 12 months to exceed the deregistration threshold of £83,000. Accordingly Omar is not required to register.

Test your understanding 3

1   Register now – taxable turnover is expected to exceed the registration threshold in the next 30 days.

2   Monitor and register later – taxable turnover for the period to date does not exceed the registration threshold.

     Note that if there has not yet been 12 months of trading, you do not time apportion the threshold. Just compare the taxable turnover of the shorter period to the full threshold.

3   Register now – taxable turnover has exceeded the registration threshold in the last 12 months.

4   Monitor and register later – taxable turnover has not exceeded the threshold.

 Test your understanding 4

1   The correct answer is D.

     Taxable turnover for the first 12 months to 31 January is £76,800, to 28 February £79,600 and to 31 March £82,400 and to 30 April £85,200.

2   The correct answer is D.

     Traders must notify HMRC within 30 days of exceeding the threshold.

 Test your understanding 5

The correct answer is B.

Two registrations are needed. One is in respect of all of Wayne's sole trade businesses, and another in respect of the partnership with his wife.

Test your understanding 6

The correct answer is B.

A is incorrect as it would be compulsory to complete VAT returns.

C is incorrect as the public would have to pay VAT which they could not recover.

D is incorrect as VAT-registered customers would have to pay VAT on purchases which they could then recover, such that the price of the goods and services to them is the same whether or not the supplier business chooses to be VAT-registered.

 Test your understanding 7

(a)   Jig Ltd must notify HMRC of their business cessation by 9 November 20X0 (i.e. within 30 days). The business will be deregistered from 10 October 20X0 (i.e. date of cessation), or from a mutually agreed later date.

(b)   Eli's registration will be cancelled with effect from 1 May 20X0 (i.e. date of request), or an agreed later date.

 Test your understanding 8

1   No – businesses that only make zero-rated supplies can apply to be exempted from registration.

2   No – if a business exceeds the registration threshold it need not register if taxable turnover in the next 12 months will be below the deregistration threshold.

3   Yes – the taxable turnover of all of a trader's sole trader businesses are aggregated to determine whether the trader has exceeded the VAT threshold.

4   No – exempt supplies are not taken into account for registration.

Test your understanding 9

1   False – if a trader fails to register when they should, then they can be asked to pay over all the output VAT they should have charged.

2   False – traders making taxable supplies can register voluntarily.

3   False – traders making only exempt supplies cannot register for VAT.

4   True – the VAT registration number must be shown on all invoices.

5   False – traders only **have to** deregister if they cease to make taxable supplies. If their supplies fall below the deregistration threshold they can choose to deregister.

 Test your understanding 10

The correct answer is C.

Ahmed must register under the future prospects test as his taxable supplies in the next 30 days will exceed the registration threshold.

He must notify HMRC by 30 June and will be registered with effect from 1 June.

VAT documentation

Introduction

This chapter looks at how VAT is collected via a VAT invoice and all the details that are required to be shown on such an invoice. Other documents such as credit notes and pro-forma invoices are also covered.

The rules for determining the tax point are important. The tax point is the date which determines in which VAT period the VAT on transactions should be included.

Finally, the importance of keeping staff up-to-date on changes in VAT legislation is discussed.

ASSESSMENT CRITERIA	CONTENTS
Identify and analyse relevant information on VAT (1.1)	1 Tax point (time of supply)
VAT invoices, required information and deadlines (1.4)	2 VAT invoices 3 Other documentation
Calculate relevant input and output tax (2.2)	4 Changes in VAT legislation
Inform the appropriate person about VAT-related matters (4.1)	

1 Tax point (time of supply)

1.1 Introduction

 Definition

The **tax point** is the date on which the liability for output tax arises. It is the date on which a supply is recorded as taking place for the purposes of the tax return. It is also referred to as the **time of supply**.

Most taxable persons complete a VAT return each quarter. The return must include all supplies whose tax points fall within that quarter.

If the rate of VAT changes then all supplies with a tax point up to the date of change will be at the old rate and all supplies on or after the date of change will be at the new rate.

1.2 The basic tax point

The **basic tax point** for goods is the date when goods are 'removed' which usually means the date of delivery of those goods or the date the customer takes the goods away.

A tax point also occurs if goods are not 'removed' but are made available to a customer – for example if a specialist installer is constructing a new machine for a customer on site in their factory, the tax point will occur when the machine is handed over and not when all the materials are delivered to the site.

For services, the tax point is the date the services are performed/ completed.

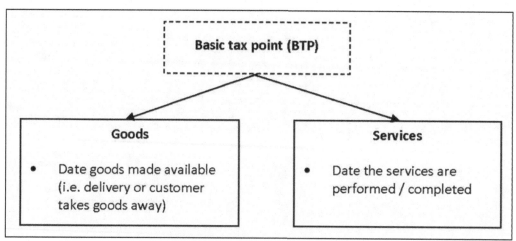

Example

Queue Ltd received an order for goods from a customer on 14 March. The goods were despatched on 18 March and the customer paid on 15 April when they received their invoice dated 13 April.

State the basic tax point date.

Solution

The tax point is 18 March (i.e. the date of despatch).

1.3 Actual tax point

The basic tax point is amended in two situations.

Earlier tax point	Later tax point
• A tax invoice is issued or a payment is received on or before the basic tax point • In these circumstances the date of invoice or payment is the time when the supply is treated as taking place	• A tax invoice is issued within 14 days after the basic tax point (14 day rule) (see section 1.4 below) • In these circumstances the date of issue of the invoice is the time when the supply is treated as taking place

Note that an invoice is not issued until it has been sent or given to the customer.

1.4 The 14 day rule

Provided that written approval is received from the local VAT office, the 14 day rule in respect of issuing tax invoices can be varied.

For example, with agreement, it can be extended to accommodate a supplier who

- usually issues all of his invoices each month on the last day of the month, and

- would like the month end invoice date to be the tax point date.

However, where applicable, always apply the 14 day rule in your assessment unless the question suggests an extension has been agreed.

Note that the 14 day rule cannot apply to invoices which are only for zero-rated goods as these are not tax invoices.

Most exports are zero-rated (see Chapter 8 for more details), so the tax point for these goods is always the earlier of:

- the supply of goods, and

- the receipt of payment.

1.5 Identification of the tax point date

The procedure to identify the actual tax point date is as follows:

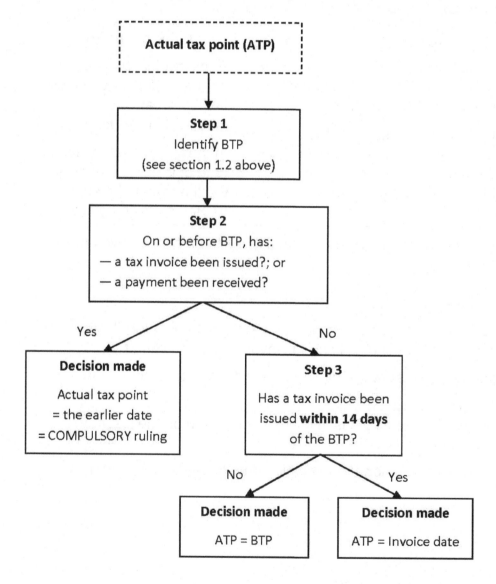

Reference material

Information about tax points is included in the indirect tax reference material provided in the real assessment, so you do not need to learn it.

It can be found in the 'Tax points' section.

You need to be familiar with the location and content of the material as in the assessment you will need to access the correct part of the reference material from a series of clickable links.

Why not look up the correct part of the indirect tax reference material in the appendix to this text book now?

1.6 Deposits received in advance

If a business receives a deposit or part payment in advance then this creates a tax point when the deposit is received.

However, this is only for the deposit, not the whole supply. The business must account for the VAT included in the deposit.

No tax point is created for a returnable deposit, where the deposit will be returned to the customer when they bring the item back safely (e.g. a deposit required to ensure the safe return of a hired item).

 Example

Ahmed receives a £60 deposit from a customer on 1 July.

The total cost of the item is £210 including VAT at 20% and the customer pays the balance of £150 on 12 September when they collect the goods.

On 15 September Ahmed issues an invoice to his customer which he marks as paid in full.

How is VAT accounted for on this transaction?

Solution

Paying the deposit of £60 created a tax point on 1 July (as the payment date is before the goods are collected).

The amount of VAT is £10 (£60 × 20/120) and this must be entered in the VAT return which includes 1 July.

When the goods were collected and paid for on 12 September this created a further tax point (as the payment date is on the same day as the goods are collected).

The VAT is £25 (£150 × 20/120) and this must be included in the VAT return which includes 12 September.

The invoice date is not important as payment was made at the time the goods were removed (i.e. on the basic tax point date).

Test your understanding 1

In each of the following cases, state the tax point date.

		Tax point
1	Goods delivered to a customer on 10 July, tax invoice sent out on 15 July and payment received 30 July.	
2	Tax invoice sent out to a customer on 12 August, goods delivered to the customer on 16 August, payment received 20 September.	
3	Payment received from customer on 4 September, goods sent to customer on 5 September with a tax invoice dated on that day.	
4	Goods delivered to a customer on 13 September, invoice sent out on 30 September and payment received 31 October.	

KAPLAN PUBLISHING

Test your understanding 2

A VAT-registered business receives a £100 non-refundable deposit on 19 October from a customer for the supply of goods which are despatched on 25 October.

The goods are invoiced on 31 October and the balance of £350 is paid on 10 November.

Both amounts are VAT-inclusive.

1 What is the tax point for the deposit?

A 19 October

B 25 October

C 31 October

D 10 November

2 What is the output VAT on the deposit?

A £20.00

B £16.66

3 What is the tax point for the balance?

A 19 October

B 25 October

C 31 October

D 10 November

4 What is the output VAT on the balance?

A £70.00

B £58.34

1.7 Continuous supplies

Some services are performed over a long period but are invoiced at regular intervals, rather than when the service has been completed (e.g. the leasing of equipment or the provision of utilities such as gas and electricity).

If services are performed on a continuous basis with payments received regularly or from time to time, there is a tax point each time there is a payment, which is the **earlier of**:

- the date a VAT invoice is issued, or

- the date a payment is received.

If payments are due to be made at regular intervals (for example, by banker's order or direct debit), a VAT invoice can be issued at the start of any period of up to one year (provided that more than one payment is due in the period) to cover all the payments due in that period.

For each payment the business should set out the following:

- VAT-exclusive amount

- date on which the payment is due

- rate of VAT

- VAT payable.

In this case the supplying business (i.e. the business issuing the invoice) does not have to pay all the output VAT to HMRC at the start of the year.

It will account for the tax on the earlier of:

- the payment due date for each regular payment, or

- the date payment is received.

The customer can reclaim input tax at the same time.

1.8 Goods on sale or return

Sometimes a customer may be sent goods on approval with a specified period in which to decide to keep the goods or return them.

Until the customer decides to keep the goods (referred to as 'adopting the goods'), they belong to the supplier and no VAT is due.

However, this situation could be exploited by giving the customer an artificially long period before they have to return or adopt the goods.

Accordingly, the tax point date rules stop goods being held for more than a year without VAT being due.

The basic tax point therefore occurs at the earliest of:

- the date the goods are adopted

- the date payment is received (except for refundable deposits)

- expiration of the time limit for adopting the goods

- 12 months from the date the goods were despatched.

Example

Reesha sells jewellery on a sale or return basis. Customers are given 90 days to decide to accept or return the goods.

Jewellery with a VAT-exclusive value of £670 is sent to Mike on 1 August 20X6. He decides to buy the goods on 28 October 20X6 and notifies Reesha on that date. Reesha receives payment from him on 7 November 20X6.

The tax point is 28 October 20X6 as this is the date the goods are adopted and is earlier than the expiry of the fixed time limit.

If Mike had not notified Reesha but simply sent the payment, then the tax point would be the 31 October 20X6 as this is the date the fixed time period expires.

 Reference material

Information about continuous supplies and goods on sale or return is included in the indirect tax reference material provided in the real assessment, so you do not need to learn it.

It can be found in the 'Tax points' section.

You need to be familiar with the location and content of the material as in the assessment you will need to access the correct part of the reference material from a series of clickable links.

Why not look up the correct part of the indirect tax reference material in the appendix to this text book now?

2 VAT invoices

2.1 Introduction

All businesses that are registered for VAT must provide evidence to VAT-registered customers of the VAT they have been charged.

In order to do this the supplier must give or send to the purchaser a VAT invoice **within 30 days** of the earlier of:

* supply of the goods or services, or
* receipt of the payment.

VAT invoices are not required:

- if the purchaser is not VAT-registered, or
- if the supply is wholly zero-rated or exempt.

In practice it is impossible to tell if a purchaser is VAT-registered or not, so traders normally issue a VAT invoice anyway, although retailers selling to the public do not have to issue a VAT invoice unless requested.

Traders will normally issue invoices for zero-rated sales which show the same details as for other supplies, but technically this is not a VAT invoice.

The original VAT invoice is sent to the customer and forms their evidence for reclaiming input VAT.

A copy must be kept by the supplier to support the calculation of output VAT.

2.2 Form of a VAT invoice

There is **no standard format for invoices**. The exact design is the choice of the business, but it must show the following details (unless the invoice is a **simplified tax invoice** that you will see later):

- identifying number which must follow a sequence (if an invoice is spoilt or cancelled it must be kept as a VAT officer may wish to inspect it)
- supplier's name and address
- supplier's VAT registration number
- the date of issue of the invoice
- the date of supply (tax point) if different from the invoice date
- name and address of customer (i.e. the person to whom the goods or services are supplied)
- type of supply
  - sale
  - hire purchase, credit sale, conditional sale or similar transaction
  - loan or exchange
  - hire, lease or rental
  - process (making goods using the customer's own materials)
  - sale on commission (e.g. an estate agent)
  - supply on sale or return
- description of the goods or services
- unit price or rate, excluding VAT

- quantity of goods or extent of services

- rate of tax and amount payable (in sterling) excluding VAT for each separate description

- total amount payable (excluding VAT) in sterling

- rate of any cash discount offered (these are also called settlement discounts)

- separate rate and amount of VAT charged for each rate of VAT

- total amount of VAT chargeable.

A VAT invoice does NOT have to include any other items such as:

- customer's order number

- date of order

- customer's VAT registration number

- method of delivery.

Invoices can be paper or electronic (e-invoice). If electronic it must be in a secure format like a pdf.

Reference material

Information about the contents of an invoice is included in the indirect tax reference material provided in the real assessment, so you do not need to learn it.

It can be found in the 'VAT invoices' section.

You need to be familiar with the location and content of the material as in the assessment you will need to access the correct part of the reference material from a series of clickable links.

Why not look up the correct part of the indirect tax reference material in the appendix to this text book now?

2.3 Exempt or zero-rated supplies

If a business issues an invoice which includes zero-rated or exempt supplies then the invoice must show clearly that there is no VAT on those items and their values must be totalled separately.

Alternatively the business could issue separate invoices for zero-rated and for exempt supplies.

Note that separate invoices for only zero-rated or exempt supplies are not tax invoices.

2.4 Example of a VAT invoice

The example invoice below shows the detail required for a valid tax invoice.

Example

MICRO TRAINING GROUP LTD
Unit 34, Castlewell Trading Estate
Manchester M12 5RHF

To: Slough Labels Ltd	Sales invoice number:	35
Station Unit	VAT registration number:	234 5566 87
Slough	Date of issue:	30 September 20X0
SL1 3EJ	Tax point:	12 September 20X0

Sales:

No.	Description and price	Amount excl VAT £ p	VAT rate	VAT £ p
6	Programmable calculators FR34 at £24.76	148.56	20%	29.71
12	Programmable calculators GT60 at £36.80	441.60	20%	88.32
		590.16		118.03
	Delivery	23.45	20%	4.69
		613.61		122.72
VAT		122.72		
TOTAL		736.33		

Terms: Net 30 days.

2.5 Rounding VAT

Usually, the amount of VAT calculated will not be a whole number of pounds and pence. You will therefore need a rounding adjustment.

In your assessment, the total amount of VAT payable on an invoice should be rounded down to the nearest penny (i.e. any fraction of a penny is ignored).

Note that in practice this rule only applies to invoice calculations (not to every calculation). Other calculations may be rounded mathematically.

Test your understanding 3

Calculate the total VAT to be charged in respect of each of the three VAT invoices below.

Invoice	Description and price	Net of VAT £ p	VAT rate	VAT £ p
1	16 × 6 metre hosepipes @ £3.23 each	51.68	20%	
2	24 × bags of compost @ £5.78 each	138.72	20%	
3	Supply of kitchen units	1,084.57	20%	

Note that retailers are not allowed to use this rounding down rule.

If they use special retail schemes then they calculate VAT as a fraction of their takings and hence are not affected by the rounding rule.

If they use till technology to calculate the VAT on each transaction and issue an invoice, then they can round each VAT calculation up or down as appropriate. The total VAT on the invoice will simply be a total of the VAT for each item.

2.6 VAT and trade or bulk buy discounts

A trader may offer a **trade discount** to loyal customers and/or a **bulk buy discount** (or bulk quantity discount).

If this is the case, VAT is charged on the **discounted price**, not the full price of the goods or services.

 Example

Joachim is in business manufacturing angle brackets which he sells to retailers.

He offers a 5% trade discount.

He sells angle brackets (a standard-rated supply) with a pre-discount price of £1,000 to Kim Ltd.

How much VAT should he charge on the invoice?

Solution

VAT should be calculated on the discounted price.

Accordingly, the VAT is £190.00 (£1,000 × 95% × 20%).

The amount of the VAT is fixed by what is on the invoice and this must be calculated on the discounted figure.

In the example above:

• The supplier's OUTPUT tax and the customer's INPUT tax is £190.00.

• The customer will need a copy of the invoice to reclaim VAT and they can only reclaim £190.00.

 Test your understanding 4

An invoice is issued for standard-rated goods with a list price of £380.00 (excluding VAT).

A 10% bulk buy discount is given.

How much VAT should be included on the invoice?

A   £76.00

B   £57.00

C   £68.40

D   £63.33

Sometimes a business will **offer to pay a customer's VAT**.

This is really just another form of discount.

VAT is calculated on the amount the customer would have paid on the discounted price, not the full price (i.e. the amount paid by the customer is treated as the VAT-inclusive amount).

 Example

XY Ltd sells beds with a normal retail price of £240 (which includes VAT of £40).

They run a promotional offer to pay the customers' VAT for them and hence the customer pays £200.

How much output VAT must XY Ltd account for?

Solution

XY Ltd must treat the £200 paid as a VAT-inclusive price and account for VAT of £33.33 (£200 × 1/6).

Test your understanding 5

Calculate the amount of output VAT that should be charged on the following invoices for standard-rated supplies.

	Output tax £ p
Pre-discounted price = £1,000 Trade discount of 10%	
Supplier offers to pay customer's VAT Amount paid = £2,500	
Pre-discounted price = £750 Bulk buy discount of 8%	

2.7 VAT and cash (prompt payment) discounts

If a trader offers a discount for payment within a certain period, then VAT must be accounted for on the **actual** amount that the customer pays.

This causes difficulty for the supplier as they do not know in advance whether the customer will pay in time and be entitled to take the discount.

There are three ways that a trader can deal with this.

(1) Invoice the customer for the full amount and charge VAT on the full amount.

   If the customer pays in time and takes the discount, then the trader can issue a credit note for the discount plus VAT.

   Note that if the VAT rate changes between the issue of the invoice and the credit note, then the original VAT rate must be used on the credit note.

(2) Invoice the customer for the discounted amount and charge VAT on the discounted amount.

   If the customer does not pay in time and therefore is not entitled to the discount, the trader can issue a supplementary invoice for the discount plus VAT.

(3) The trader can invoice for the full amount plus VAT but include on the invoice information about the discounted amount plus VAT.

   The customer then knows how much to pay if they make payment within the discount period.

   It must be made clear on the invoice that the customer can only recover the input tax that they have actually paid.

   A warning should be included that claiming more VAT than they are entitled to is an offence.

Example

Perry Ltd offers customers a 5% cash discount if they pay within 30 days. The company invoices customers the full amount and then issues a credit note for any discount.

Perry Ltd sells standard-rated goods worth £670 VAT-exclusive to Evans. Evans pays within 30 days so is entitled to the 5% discount.

Perry Ltd should invoice Evans for £804 (£670 plus £134 VAT at 20%).

They should then issue a credit note for £40.20 (£33.50 (5% of £670) plus of £6.70 VAT at 20%).

Perry Ltd must account for output VAT of £127.30 (£134.00 – £6.70). Evans can recover input VAT of £127.30.

Note that in an assessment, if you are just asked to calculate the discounted amount and the VAT, there is no need to do it in two stages.

You can calculate just as you do with trade and bulk buy discounts (i.e. input VAT recoverable = (£670 × 95% × 20%) = £127.30)

 Test your understanding 6

A trader issues an invoice to a customer for the following:

– standard-rated items of £220 plus VAT

– zero-rated items of £130

A cash discount of 2% is available and is given through a credit note.

Assuming the customer takes the cash discount, how much input VAT will they be entitled to claim on the invoice less the credit note?

A   £44.00

B   £43.12

C   £36.66

D   £35.93

Reference material

Information about discounts is included in the indirect tax reference material provided in the real assessment, so you do not need to learn it.

It can be found in the 'VAT invoices' section.

You need to be familiar with the location and content of the material as in the assessment you will need to access the correct part of the reference material from a series of clickable links.

Why not look up the correct part of the indirect tax reference material in the appendix to this text book now?

2.8 Simplified (or less detailed) VAT invoices

Invoices with fewer details on them can be issued by any business, if the value of the supply is below a certain limit.

If the total amount of the supply **(including VAT)** does not exceed £250, then the business may issue a simplified invoice.

However, a full VAT invoice must be issued if a customer requests one.

The details required on the simplified invoice are:

- supplier's name and address
- supplier's VAT registration number
- date of supply (tax point)
- description sufficient to identify the goods or services
- amount payable (including VAT) for each rate
- the VAT rate applicable.

The main differences between the less detailed invoice and full invoice are that the customer's name and address can be omitted, and the total on the invoice includes the VAT without the VAT itself being shown separately.

Although this invoice shows less detail, it is still a valid tax invoice.

This means that if the purchaser is a VAT-registered business they can use the invoice to support a claim for input VAT.

Example

Delta Office Supplies
46, Central Mall, Glastonbury, Somerset
G34 7QT
Telephone: 01392 43215
15 April 20X0

1 box of 50 blank DVD-R
Total including VAT @ 20%   £25.85

VAT registration number: 653 7612 44

If the business accepts credit cards they can use the sales voucher given to the cardholder as a less detailed invoice.

However, it must still contain the details above.

Exempt supplies must **not** be included in a less detailed invoice.

 Test your understanding 7

Look at the following list of items.

Select by entering the appropriate number whether the items:

1   Should only be shown on a normal detailed VAT invoice; or

2   Should be shown on both a normal detailed VAT invoice and on a less detailed invoice; or

3   Should not be shown on either form of invoice.

	Item	Number (1, 2, or 3)
A	Identifying number	
B	Tax point date	
C	Delivery date	
D	Total amount of VAT payable	
E	Customer's registration number	

Test your understanding 8

A manufacturing business which is registered for VAT sells both standard and zero-rated goods.

Which one of the following combinations of supplies can be shown on a simplified invoice?

	Standard-rated supplies	Zero-rated supplies
A	£200 + VAT	£30
B	£240 + VAT	Nil
C	£50 + VAT	£180

 Reference material

Information about simplified invoices is included in the indirect tax reference material provided in the real assessment, so you do not need to learn it.

It can be found in the 'VAT invoices' section.

You need to be familiar with the location and content of the material as in the assessment you will need to access the correct part of the reference material from a series of clickable links.

Why not look up the correct part of the indirect tax reference material in the appendix to this text book now?

2.9 Retention of invoices

All businesses must keep records of:

- all sales invoices issued except copies of the simplified VAT invoices for items under £250 (including VAT)

- all purchase invoices for items purchased for business purposes unless the gross value of the supply is £25 or less, and the purchase was from a coin-operated telephone or vending machine, or for car parking charges or tolls.

3 Other documentation

3.1 Credit notes

When customers return goods which were taxable supplies, the supplier may issue a credit note. This has to have similar information to that found on the original invoice and must be **clearly labelled as a credit note**.

The number and date of the original tax invoice should also appear on the credit note.

If the supplier issues the credit note without making a VAT adjustment, the credit note must say '**This is not a credit note for VAT**'.

A supplier is not allowed to issue a credit note to recover VAT on bad debts (i.e. irrecoverable debts).

From the supplier's point of view the VAT on the credit note issued must be deducted from output VAT payable.

From the customer's point of view the VAT on the credit note received must be deducted from input tax recoverable.

Alternatively the supplier can cancel the original invoice and reissue it with the correct figures.

 Test your understanding 9

A business issues a sales credit note.

What is the effect on output VAT?

A   Output VAT will increase

B   Output VAT will decrease

C   Input VAT will increase

D   Input VAT will decrease

3.2 Debit notes

If a customer returns goods they can wait for:

- the supplier to reissue a corrected invoice, or

- the supplier to issue them with a credit note, or

- they can issue a debit note to their supplier.

Note that these are **alternatives** – you **cannot** account for both a debit note issued and a credit note received for the same supply.

From the supplier's point of view the VAT on a debit note received from a customer must be deducted from output tax payable.

From the customer's point of view the VAT on a debit note issued must be deducted from their input tax recoverable.

The treatment of the VAT can be summarised as follows:

	SELLER (supplier)	BUYER (customer)
Seller issues credit note	Deduct from output tax	Deduct from input tax
Buyer issues debit note	Deduct from output tax	Deduct from input tax
Effect	Reduce VAT payable	Increase VAT payable

 Test your understanding 10

A business issues a purchase debit note.

What is the effect on their VAT?

A   Output VAT will increase

B   Output VAT will decrease

C   Input VAT will increase

D   Input VAT will decrease

 Reference material

Information about debit and credit notes is included in the indirect tax reference material provided in the real assessment, so you do not need to learn it.

It can be found in the 'VAT invoices' section.

You need to be familiar with the location and content of the material as in the assessment you will need to access the correct part of the reference material from a series of clickable links.

Why not look up the correct part of the indirect tax reference material in the appendix to this text book now?

3.3 Pro-forma invoices

When a business issues a sales invoice that includes VAT, the VAT becomes payable to HMRC next time the business submits a return.

A business is therefore unlikely to issue a tax invoice before goods are despatched. This can cause cash flow problems if the customer has not yet paid the invoice, because the business then has to pay the VAT to HMRC before collecting it from their customers.

To avoid this, a business may issue a **pro-forma invoice** for goods or services not yet supplied, which essentially is an offer to supply goods and services and a request for payment.

Once the customer accepts the goods or services offered and/or a payment is received, the business will then issue a 'live' tax invoice to replace the pro-forma.

Because a pro-forma invoice does not rank as a VAT invoice the supplier is not required to pay VAT to HMRC until the 'live' tax invoice is issued.

For this reason, the customer cannot reclaim VAT on a pro-forma invoice but must instead wait until the valid VAT invoice is received.

Pro-forma invoices must be clearly marked with the words '**This is not a VAT invoice**'.

Test your understanding 11

Which of the following statements about pro-forma invoices are FALSE?

Enter a tick in the final box for each false statement.

		False
A	A pro-forma invoice IS a valid tax invoice	
B	A pro-forma invoice IS NOT a valid tax invoice	
C	A customer receiving a pro-forma invoice can use it to reclaim the input tax shown	
D	A pro-forma invoice is really just an offer to supply goods and services and a request for payment	

Reference material

Information about pro-forma invoices is included in the indirect tax reference material provided in the real assessment, so you do not need to learn it.

It can be found under the heading of 'Pro-forma invoices' in the 'VAT invoices' section.

You need to be familiar with the location and content of the material as in the assessment you will need to access the correct part of the reference material from a series of clickable links.

Why not look up the correct part of the indirect tax reference material in the appendix to this text book now?

 Test your understanding 12

Refer to the three invoices set out below which have been received from suppliers during March 20X8. No entries have yet been made in Hoddle Ltd's books of account in respect of these 3 documents.

You are required to state whether these are valid VAT tax invoices and how much input tax (if any) can be claimed in respect of these.

Engineering Supplies Limited

Haddlefield Road, Blaysley, CG6 6AW
Tel/Fax: 01376 44531

Hoddle Limited
22 Formguard Street
Pexley
PY6 3QW

SALES INVOICE NO: 2155

Date: 27 March 20X8

	£
VAT omitted in error from invoice no 2139 dated 15 March 20X8	
£2,667.30 @ 20%	533.46
Total due	533.46

Terms: net 30 days

VAT registration: 318 1827 58

Alpha Stationery

Aindsale Centre, Mexton, EV1 4DF
Telephone: 01392 43215

26 March 20X8

1 box transparent folders : red

Total incl VAT @ 20%	14.84
Amount tendered	20.00
Change	5.16

VAT registration: 356 7612 33

JAMIESON & CO

Jamieson House, Baines Road, Gresham, GM7 2PQ
Telephone: 01677 35567   Fax: 01677 57640

PRO-FORMA SALES INVOICE

VAT registration: 412 7553 67

Hoddle Limited
22 Formguard Street
Pexley
PY6 3QW

For professional services in connection with debt collection

	£
Our fees	350.00
VAT	70.00
Total due	420.00

A VAT invoice will be submitted when the total due is paid in full.

	Valid VAT invoice	Input tax £ p
Engineering Supplies Ltd	YES/NO	
Alpha Stationery	YES/NO	
Jamieson and Co	YES/NO	

3.4 Statements and demands for payment

It is important to appreciate that only VAT invoices and credit notes should be entered in the VAT records.

When a business sends out a demand for payment or a statement there is no VAT implication.

VAT has already been recorded and the demand or statement is simply the business trying to collect what it is owed.

3.5 Orders and delivery notes

These are also ignored for VAT and cannot be used by a customer as evidence for reclaiming VAT on their purchases.

3.6 VAT-only invoices

Sometimes a business needs to increase VAT charged on an earlier invoice or may have forgotten to include VAT.

One solution would be to credit the original invoice and then re-invoice it.

Alternatively the business can issue an invoice just for the VAT and label it as a VAT-only invoice.

Such an invoice must be entered in the VAT records and the tax paid over to HMRC as usual.

A registered purchaser who receives the invoice will treat it as a normal VAT invoice and be able to recover the VAT charged.

 4 Changes in VAT legislation

4.1 Change in the rate of VAT

The tax point date becomes very important when there is a change in the rate of VAT or if a supply is reclassified from one rate of VAT to another.

Tax invoices with a tax point date before the change must use the old rate of VAT.

If they have a date on/after the change then they must use the new rate.

4.2 Effect of a VAT rate change on a business

A change in the rate of VAT has a major effect on the business accounting system including the following:

- Sales invoices need to be produced with the correct rate of VAT.

- Sales prices used in quotes or for pricing invoices must include the correct rate of VAT.

- Retail businesses need to make sure that prices displayed to the public are correct.

- Staff expense claims must reclaim the correct rate of VAT on (for example) mileage expenses.

- The correct input tax reclaim must be made for purchases and expenses.

  Input VAT claimed should be whatever figure is shown on the invoice for the purchase or expense.

  However, staff would need to know the details of any rate change so that they can query any actual errors with suppliers.

In a computerised system the accounting software must be updated to produce sales invoices at the correct rate and to deal with differing rates of VAT on purchase invoices.

If the VAT is calculated at the point of sale by a till system, the system must be adjusted to take account of the new rate.

In both cases it is important that the change occurs at the correct time. For example, new prices would need to be quoted to customers from the date of change.

However, sales invoices must use the rate of VAT relevant to the tax point date and not necessarily the date the invoice is raised.

4.3 Changing prices

Whether or not a change in VAT rate is passed on to the customer is a commercial decision for a business to make.

The current prices can be maintained and the cost of a VAT increase (or profit from a VAT decrease) can be absorbed by the business.

If the rate of VAT increases and the business does not pass on the increase to their customers then they will have reduced cash flow as well as profit.

The opposite would be true if the VAT rate decreased and the business did not pass on the reduction to their customers.

4.4 Informing staff

A number of different staff within a business would need to be told about a rate change and its effects.

- IT department staff – to ensure the relevant changes are made to the computerised accounting system.

- Sales ledger staff – to raise or check sales invoices correctly.

- Purchase ledger staff – so that they can check purchase invoices correctly.

- Sales staff – to ensure customers are given correct prices.

- Marketing department staff – so that any new brochures or publicity material is correct.

- Staff generally – to ensure their expense claims are made correctly.

In your assessment you may need to complete an email advising relevant people of the change, as shown in the following hypothetical example.

Example

To:	Sales ledger staff
From:	Junior Accountant
Subject:	Change in the rate of VAT
Date:	14/3/20X0

Please note that the standard rate of VAT which applies to all our products will change on 1 April 20X0 from 20% to 22%.

Any invoices with a tax point date of 1 April or later must have the new VAT rate applied.

It is important that invoices with a tax point date before 1 April continue to include VAT at the old rate.

---

5   Test your understanding

Test your understanding 13

Indicate whether the following statements are true or false.
Tick one box on each line

		True	*False*
1	Traders do not have to supply a VAT invoice unless their customer is VAT-registered.		
2	Businesses can issue less detailed VAT invoices if the total amount of the supply, excluding VAT, does not exceed £250.		
3	The VAT invoice is used by a customer as their evidence for reclaiming input VAT.		
4	A VAT invoice must be issued to a customer within 30 days of the tax point.		

Test your understanding 14

In each of the following cases, state the tax point date.

		Tax point
1	Goods delivered to a customer on 15 August, invoice sent out on 20 August and payment received 30 August.	
2	Pro-forma invoice issued 3 June, payment received 10 June, and goods delivered 30 June with a tax invoice dated on that day.	
3	Goods delivered to a customer on 4 March, invoice sent out on 25 March and payment received 15 April.	
4	Invoice sent to a customer on 10 December, goods delivered 18 December and payment received 27 December.	

6 Summary

This chapter has covered two important areas for VAT – invoicing and tax points.

The tax point for a supply of goods is important as this determines the VAT period in which the VAT on those goods is included. The basic tax point is the date on which goods are delivered or collected by a customer but there are also situations in which the tax point can be earlier or later. These rules must be understood.

The special rules for continuous supplies and goods on sale or return must also be understood.

Dealing with VAT and discounts is an important area.

VAT invoices must include certain details and in normal circumstances must be given or sent to a VAT-registered purchaser. In practice this means that all purchasers will be provided with a VAT invoice whether or not they are registered. However retailers do not need to issue invoices unless a customer requests an invoice.

All businesses can issue less detailed invoices if the VAT-inclusive value of the supply is £250 or less.

Credit notes sent out by a business must include the same details as the invoice.

Pro-forma invoices must not include VAT.

Changes in the rate of VAT have a major impact on a business' recording system and possibly its cash flow and you should be able to report this.

Test your understanding answers

Test your understanding 1

1   15 July – invoice within 14 days after basic tax point
    (i.e. the delivery date 10 July)

2   12 August – goods invoiced before delivery

3   4 September – payment received before delivery

4   13 September – delivery date

Test your understanding 2

1   The correct answer is A.
    Receipt of cash on 19 October creates a tax point.

2   The correct answer is B.
    £100 is VAT-inclusive so the VAT element is £16.66 (£100 × 1/6)

3   The correct answer is C.
    The goods are invoiced within 14 days of delivery so a later tax
    point is created.

4   The correct answer is B.
    Total VAT = (£450 × 1/6) = £75.00
    VAT on balancing payment = (£75.00 – £16.66 above) = £58.34

Test your understanding 3

1   VAT on 6 metre hosepipes = £10.33 (£51.68 × 20% = £10.336)

2   VAT on bags of compost = £27.74 (£138.72 × 20% = £27.744)

3   VAT on kitchen units = £216.91 (£1,084.57 × 20% = £216.914)

All rounded down to the nearest penny.

Test your understanding 4

The correct answer is C.

	£ p
List price of goods	380.00
Less: 10% trade discount	(38.00)
Amount on which VAT to be calculated	342.00
VAT (20% × £342.00)	68.40
Alternative calculation:	
VAT = (£380.00 × 90%) at 20%	68.40

Test your understanding 5

VAT must be charged on the price payable after discount.

£180.00 ((£1,000 − 10% of £1,000) = £900 × 20%)

£416.66 (£2,500 × 20/120) rounded down

£138.00 (£750 − 8% of £750) × 20%

Test your understanding 6

The correct answer is B.

The invoice will show £220 plus VAT of £44 (20% of £220)

The credit note will show discount of £4.40 (2% of £220) plus VAT of £0.88 (20% of £4.40)

This gives net VAT of £43.12 (£44 − £0.88)

VAT must be charged only on the standard-rated supplies. There is no VAT on zero-rated items so they are ignored in this calculation.

Note that the VAT could have been calculated directly as:

£43.12 ((£220 − 2% of £220) × 20%), or
£43.12 (£220 × 98% × 20%)

Test your understanding 7

A   1

B   2

C   3

D   1

E   3

 Test your understanding 8

The correct answer is C.

The **VAT-inclusive** value of supplies on a simplified invoice cannot exceed £250.

 Test your understanding 9

The correct answer is B.

A sales credit note cancels out a sale thus reducing the sales, or outputs, of the business and consequently reducing the output VAT of the business.

 Test your understanding 10

The correct answer is D.

A purchase debit note cancels out a purchase thus reducing the purchases, or inputs, of the business and consequently reducing the input VAT of the business.

Test your understanding 11

A and C are false.

A pro-forma invoice is NOT a valid tax invoice, nor is it evidence that allows the customer to reclaim input tax.

Test your understanding 12

Engineering Supplies Ltd

This invoice is a valid VAT invoice which should be processed as a March input.

The input VAT of £533.46 can be reclaimed in the quarter to 31 March 20X8.

Alpha Stationery

This is a valid less detailed VAT invoice which should also be processed as a March input.

The VAT of £2.47 (£14.84 × 20/120) can be reclaimed in the quarter to 31 March 20X8.

Jamieson and Co

This is a pro-forma invoice so cannot be treated as a March input.

The VAT cannot be reclaimed until a valid VAT invoice is received.

Test your understanding 13

1   True – it is only compulsory to issue VAT invoices to registered traders.

2   False – the £250 is VAT-inclusive.

3   True – VAT invoices form the evidence for the reclaim of input tax.

4   True

Test your understanding 14

1   20 August.

The invoice is raised within 14 days of the delivery date (the basic tax point) and hence a later tax point is created.

2   10 June.

The issue of the pro-forma invoice is ignored so the receipt of payment is the tax point (as payment is received before delivery).

3   4 March.

The invoice is raised more than 14 days after the delivery date so the tax point remains the delivery date.

4   10 December.

The goods are invoiced before delivery so this creates an earlier tax point.

Input and output tax

Introduction

This chapter deals with some of the special rules for recovering input tax and charging output tax.

It also explains what happens when a business makes both taxable and exempt supplies and is therefore partially-exempt.

ASSESSMENT CRITERIA	CONTENTS
Calculate relevant input and output tax (2.2)	1 Recovery of input tax 2 Output tax – capital assets 3 Partial exemption

1 Recovery of input tax

1.1 Conditions

Input VAT is usually recoverable by registered traders on goods and services which are supplied to them. In order to recover the input tax the following conditions must be met:

- The goods or services must be supplied for business purposes. Traders cannot recover input VAT on items bought for personal use.

- A VAT invoice is usually needed to support the claim.

- The input VAT must not be 'blocked' (i.e. irrecoverable).

Note that there is no distinction between revenue and capital expenditure for VAT.

Input VAT can be recovered on purchases of capital assets as well as revenue expenditure provided the conditions above are satisfied.

1.2 Irrecoverable (blocked) input VAT

Input VAT on the following goods and services cannot be recovered:

- Most forms of business entertaining.

- Purchase of cars, unless they are 100% used for business purposes (e.g. car owned by a driving school purely used to give driving lessons, a taxi or a pool car used by employees).

  However, VAT can be recovered on the purchase of commercial vehicles like vans and lorries.

1.3 Business entertaining

In general a business cannot recover input VAT on entertaining. However, there are some cases where VAT on entertaining **can** be recovered.

- Employee entertaining (e.g. staff parties, staff outings and team building events).

  If non-employees are included, the business can only recover input VAT on the proportion of the expenses that relate to:

  – employees, and

  – non-employees who are customers from overseas.

- VAT on entertaining overseas customers can be recovered.

Reference material

Information about VAT on vehicles and entertainment expenses is included in the indirect tax reference material provided in the real assessment, so you do not need to learn it.

It can be found in the 'Vehicles and motoring expenses' and 'Entertainment expenses' sections.

You need to be familiar with the location and content of the material as in the assessment you will need to access the correct part of the reference material from a series of clickable links.

Why not look up the correct part of the indirect tax reference material in the appendix to this text book now?

Test your understanding 1

You are given the following information about business costs for the quarter to 31.12.X1.

Complete the table to show the amount of input tax that can be reclaimed on each item (to the nearest pence).

All items are standard-rated for VAT purposes.

	Item	VAT-inclusive cost £ p	Input tax recoverable £ p
1	Car to be used by the managing director 60% for business and 40% privately	16,600.00	
2	Delivery van	17,500.00	
3	Staff party – staff were each allowed to bring a guest. Half the cost is estimated to be for these guests	630.00	
4	Entertaining UK customers and suppliers	526.00	
5	Car to be used as a pool car (i.e. available for all employees and kept at the business premises)	11,475.00	

Test your understanding 2

You are given the following information about purchases and expenses of a manufacturing business in the quarter to 30.6.X1.

Select Yes or No in the final column to show if the input tax on each item can be reclaimed.

Description	Input VAT £ p	Reclaim input VAT?
Car – for personal use by employee	1,960.00	Yes/No
Overseas customer entertainment	235.50	Yes/No
Staff party	142.70	Yes/No
Office supplies	27.45	Yes/No
Lorry	4,000.00	Yes/No

1.4 Motor expenses

Even though businesses cannot usually recover input VAT on the purchase cost of a car, a business can recover input VAT incurred on the running costs of a car such as fuel and repairs.

This applies even when there is some private use of the car.

When a business pays fuel costs for an employee or sole trader, and there is some private use of the vehicle, extra output tax will be payable.

This extra output tax is called a **fuel scale charge** and varies with the CO_2 emissions of the car. The fuel scale charge is a **VAT-inclusive figure** so the VAT element is calculated as 1/6. However, the scale charge tables supplied by HMRC do this calculation for you.

Note that the scale charges are given in 5 g/km intervals. If a car has an emission figure which is not exactly equal to one of the scale charges on the list, then it has to be rounded down to the next lower figure.

Example

Forge Ltd provides a company car to Charles and pays for all his private fuel. The CO_2 emission level of the car is 204 g/km.

The scale charge table shows (for a 3 month period):

200 g/km	£421	VAT £70.17
205 g/km	£436	VAT £72.67

What is the output VAT payable per quarter by Forge Ltd?

Solution

The scale figure for 200 g/km is used as 204 g/km is rounded down to the nearest 5 g/km.

The VAT-exclusive amount of £350.83 (£421 – £70.17) will be added to the total outputs on the company's VAT return (see Chapter 7) and additional output tax of £70.17 will be payable by the company.

If a business does not want to pay a fuel scale charge then they can either:

(a)   reclaim only VAT on business fuel (detailed records of business and private mileage need to be kept to prove the business mileage), or

(b)   not claim any VAT on fuel at all even for commercial vehicles. This has the advantage of being simple and is useful if mileage is low.

Reference material

Information about VAT on road fuel is included in the indirect tax reference material provided in the real assessment, so you do not need to learn it.

It can be found in the 'Vehicles and motoring expenses' section.

You need to be familiar with the location and content of the material as in the assessment you will need to access the correct part of the reference material from a series of clickable links.

Why not look up the correct part of the indirect tax reference material in the appendix to this text book now?

Test your understanding 3

Scott Ltd provides a car to an employee who uses it for both private and business use. All running expenses of the car are paid for by the company including fuel.

Which one of the following statements is true?

A   There are no VAT implications

B   The company can recover all of the input tax on the running costs and need take no further action

C   The company can recover all of the input tax on the running costs of the car and must add an amount to output tax determined by a scale charge

D   The company cannot recover input tax on running costs of the car but must add an amount to output tax determined by a scale charge

2   Output tax – capital assets

2.1   Introduction

Registered traders must charge output tax on all taxable supplies at the appropriate rate. This includes sales of capital assets as well as normal revenue sales.

2.2   Sales of capital assets

Normally when a registered trader sells a capital asset they will charge VAT at the standard rate on the sale price.

However if the asset is a car on which the input tax was blocked (i.e. the trader could not recover the input tax), then no output VAT is charged as it is an exempt sale.

If the input VAT was recoverable on the car, then output VAT is charged on the sale price as normal.

Test your understanding 4

You are given the following information about sales of capital assets in the quarter to 31.12.X1.

Complete the table to show the amount of output tax that must be charged on each item (to the nearest pence).

Item	Input tax recovered	Sale proceeds (excl VAT) £	Output tax £ p
Van	Yes	11,000	
Car (1)	Yes	9,500	
Car (2)	No	10,550	
Machinery	Yes	21,000	

 Test your understanding 5

You are given the following information about sales of capital assets in the quarter to 31.12.X1.

Complete the table to show the amount of output tax that must be charged on each item (to the nearest pence).

Item	Input tax recovered	Sale proceeds (excl VAT) £	Output tax £ p
Computer	Yes	2,100	
Car	No	10,000	
Van	Yes	12,500	
Motorcycle	Yes	6,760	

3 Partial exemption

3.1 Partial exemption

A taxable person who makes both taxable supplies and exempt supplies is referred to as a **partially-exempt** trader. For this purpose it does not matter if the taxable supplies are standard or zero-rated.

The problem with partial exemption is that taxable supplies entitle the supplier to a credit for input tax in respect of related costs, whereas exempt supplies do not.

It is therefore necessary to apportion input tax between taxable and exempt supplies using a method set out by HMRC.

The most common method used is to divide input tax into three parts:

- Relating wholly to taxable supplies – all recoverable

- Relating wholly to exempt supplies – irrecoverable (but see below)

- Relating to overheads – proportion which relate to taxable supplies can be recovered, leaving the rest irrecoverable (but see below).

If the total irrecoverable input tax is no more than a certain amount, the **de minimis amount**, then it **can** be recovered.

 Example

Javid's business makes both taxable and exempt supplies. In his latest VAT period taxable supplies amounted to 60% of total supplies whilst exempt supplies made up the other 40%.

In the same period input tax of £55,770 was analysed as follows:

Relating to taxable supplies   £31,450 (recoverable)
Relating to exempt supplies   £13,780 (irrecoverable)
Relating to overheads   £10,540 (partly recoverable)

The input VAT relating to overheads is split 60% (£6,324) recoverable and 40% (£4,216) irrecoverable.

The recoverable input tax is £37,774 (£31,450 + £6,324).

The irrecoverable input tax is £17,996 (£13,780 + £4,216).

If this were below the de minimis limit it could be recovered.

Note that you will not be expected to calculate the de minimis limit.

Reference material

Information about partial-exemption is included in the indirect tax reference material provided in the real assessment, so you do not need to learn it.

It can be found in the 'Exempt and partly-exempt businesses' section.

You need to be familiar with the location and content of the material as in the assessment you will need to access the correct part of the reference material from a series of clickable links.

Why not look up the correct part of the indirect tax reference material in the appendix to this text book now?

 Test your understanding 6

A business supplies goods that are a mixture of standard-rated and exempt. Which one of the following statements is true?

A   All of the input VAT can be reclaimed

B   None of the input VAT can be reclaimed

C   All of the input VAT can be reclaimed provided certain de minimis conditions are met

D   Only the input VAT on goods and services purchased for use in making standard-rated supplies can ever be reclaimed

4   Summary

This chapter has looked at the rules for recovering input tax and examined the items which have a restricted recovery.

Cars with some private use and business entertaining are the examples of 'blocked' input tax that you are required to know for your assessment. There are some exceptions for entertaining.

The treatment of motor expenses is also an important area and you should be aware of the different treatments possible.

Finally the chapter deals with the topic of partially-exempt businesses. Such businesses may have to restrict the amount of input tax they can recover.

Test your understanding answers

Test your understanding 1

1   None – the car is not used 100% for business

2   £2,916.66 (£17,500.00 × 1/6) (round down to nearest penny)

3   £52.50 (£630.00 ÷ 2 × 1/6) VAT is recoverable on half the cost

4   None – blocked VAT

5   £1,912.50 (£11,475.00 × 1/6) – car is used 100% for business

Test your understanding 2

Car – No, reclaim of input tax if there is some private use of the car

Overseas customer entertainment – Yes, input tax is recoverable

Staff party – Yes, input tax is recoverable

Office supplies – Yes, input tax is recoverable

Lorry – Yes, input tax is recoverable on commercial vehicles

Test your understanding 3

The correct answer is C.

When a business supplies a car to an employee who uses the car at least partly privately, and pays for fuel, then the business can recover the input VAT on running costs including the fuel.

However, the company must account for output tax determined by a table of scale charges.

Test your understanding 4

Van	£2,200.00 (£11,000 × 20%)
Car 1	£1,900.00 (£9,500 × 20%)
Car 2	Nil – this is an exempt supply because the business was not able to recover the input tax on the purchase.
Machinery	£4,200.00 (£21,000 × 20%)

 Test your understanding 5

Computer	£420.00 (£2,100 × 20%)
Car	Nil – sale of a car on which the input tax was not recoverable is an exempt supply.
Van	£2,500.00 (£12,500 × 20%)
Motorcycle	£1,352.00 (£6,760 × 20%)

 Test your understanding 6

The correct answer is C.

A partially-exempt business has to apportion input tax in proportion to the levels of taxable and exempt supplies.

However, if the exempt input tax is below the de minimis amount the whole of the input tax can be recovered.

VAT accounting schemes

5

Introduction

This chapter deals with VAT accounting. There are several special schemes available for small businesses. These schemes have a number of advantages. They can reduce administration (annual accounting and flat rate scheme) or improve cash flow (cash accounting).

You should pay particular attention to which businesses are eligible and the reasons why a business might join one of these schemes.

ASSESSMENT CRITERIA	CONTENTS
Describe the VAT registration, scheme choice and deregistration requirements (1.3)	1 Normal scheme 2 Annual accounting 3 Cash accounting 4 The flat rate scheme
Complete and submit a VAT return and make any associated payment within statutory time limits (2.5)	
Communicate information about VAT due to or from the tax authority (4.2)	

1 Normal scheme

1.1 Return periods

When a business is first registered it automatically joins the normal (standard) VAT scheme. If the business wishes to make use of any of the special accounting schemes described below then it must apply to do so.

In the normal scheme, all registered traders have to complete a VAT return every return period. Information to complete the return is taken from sales and purchase information – usually from the VAT account compiled from the original and verified daybook totals. Any amounts of VAT due must be paid over to HMRC or a claim made for VAT to be reimbursed.

Return periods are normally 3 months.

1.2 Submission of returns

All traders (with a few exceptions) must submit their returns online, and pay their VAT electronically.

Returns must normally be submitted to **arrive with HMRC** within one month and seven days after the end of the return period.

Traders who are allowed to submit paper returns must ensure that they arrive with HMRC within one month after the end of the return period.

Completion of VAT returns is dealt with in Chapter 7.

1.3 Payment of VAT

Electronic payments **must** be made if returns are submitted online and **may** be made when paper returns are submitted.

The payment date is **one month and seven days after the end of the return period**.

The extra 7 days does not apply:

- if the trader uses the annual accounting scheme

- if the trader has to make monthly payments (compulsory for large businesses).

Postal payments are rare as they can only be made with paper VAT returns. Payment is due at the same time as the return (i.e. payments must have cleared HMRC bank account by **one month after the end of the return period)**.

Example

Jonas has a quarterly return period to 30 April.

If Jonas submits a paper VAT return it must be with HMRC by 31 May. If he submits electronically he will have until 7 June to submit.

If Jonas submits a paper return he can send a cheque with his return to clear HMRC's bank account by 31 May. Otherwise he must pay electronically by 7 June.

If a trader pays by direct debit the payment is taken by HMRC from the trader's account three working days after the extra 7 day period allowed for electronic payments.

Other electronic payment methods include:

- By debit or credit card over the internet

- Telephone banking payments

- BACS direct credit

- Bank Giro.

 Test your understanding 1

Oak Ltd has prepared its VAT return for the quarter ended 30 September.

1   When is Oak Ltd's return due assuming it does not submit its returns electronically?

    A   14 October

    B   30 October

    C   31 October

    D   7 November

2   What would be the due date for submission of the return if Oak Ltd submitted it electronically?

A   14 October

B   31 October

C   6 November

D   7 November

3   Assuming Oak Ltd submits its return electronically and pays by direct debit, when will HMRC take the money from Oak Ltd's bank account?

A   The same date as the return is due

B   3 days after the return is due

C   3 working days after the return is due

Reference material

Information about submission and payment dates is included in the indirect tax reference material provided in the real assessment, so you do not need to learn it.

It can be found in the 'VAT periods, submitting returns and paying VAT' section.

You need to be familiar with the location and content of the material as in the assessment you will need to access the correct part of the reference material from a series of clickable links.

Why not look up the correct part of the indirect tax reference material in the appendix to this text book now?

1.4   Refunds of VAT

If the business has more input tax than output tax in a particular VAT period then it will be due a refund.

Before making a repayment HMRC makes additional checks on the return to ensure the claim is valid.

Provided the additional checks confirm a repayment is due, the repayment is automatically made directly into the trader's bank account.

In most cases this will be within 10 working days of receiving the return.

Traders who regularly receive repayments can choose to submit monthly returns.

A refund will not be made automatically if there is an outstanding debt due to HMRC.

1.5 Other schemes

There are a number of special schemes for accounting for VAT. These are designed to help small businesses by reducing administration and may improve cash flow.

The schemes which you must know about are:

- annual accounting
- cash accounting
- the flat rate scheme.

Note that all of the schemes are optional to join and are subject to conditions.

There are also special schemes for retailers and businesses that sell second-hand goods. However you do not need to know details of these.

2 Annual accounting

2.1 Purpose of the scheme

Smaller businesses may find it costly or inconvenient to prepare the normal four quarterly VAT returns.

An 'annual' accounting scheme is available whereby a single VAT return is filed for a 12-month period (normally the accounting period of the business). This helps relieve the burden of administration.

2.2   How the scheme works

Only one VAT return is submitted each year, but VAT payments must still be made regularly.

The scheme works as follows:

*   The annual return must be filed within **2 months** of the end of the annual return period.

*   Normally, nine payments on account of the VAT liability for the year are made at the end of months 4 to 12 of the year. Each payment represents 10% of the VAT liability for the previous year.

*   A new business will base its payments on an estimate of the VAT liability for the year.

*   A balancing payment or repayment is made when the annual return is filed.

*   All payments must be made electronically with **no 7 days extension**.

*   Additional payments can be made by the business when desired.

2.3   Conditions for the annual accounting scheme

The scheme is aimed at smaller businesses and it is optional to join, however conditions need to be satisfied to be eligible to join.

*   Businesses can join the scheme provided their taxable turnover (excluding VAT and the sale of capital assets) expected in the next 12 months is no more than £1,350,000.

*   The business must be up-to-date with its VAT returns. However a business does not need a history of VAT returns to join. It can join the scheme from the day it registers.

*   Businesses must leave the scheme if their estimated taxable turnover (excluding VAT) for the next 12 months is more than £1,600,000.

    If a business takes over another business as a going concern, the estimated taxable turnover (excluding VAT) of the new combined business for the next 12 months must be assessed and compared to the £1,600,000 threshold to decide whether the business should immediately leave the scheme.

2.4 Who might use the scheme?

The scheme is useful to businesses that want to:

- reduce administration because only one VAT return is needed instead of four, and businesses have two months to prepare the return instead of the usual one month

- fix their VAT payments in advance, at least for their nine monthly or three quarterly payments. This is useful for budgeting cash flow.

It is not useful if:

- the business receives repayments as only one repayment per year will be received.

- the business taxable turnover decreases, as then the interim payments might be higher than under the standard scheme and the business will have to wait until they submit the annual VAT return to get any repayment due.

 Test your understanding 2

Jump Ltd applies to use the annual accounting scheme from 1 January 20X1. The company's net VAT liability for the year ended 31 December 20X0 was £3,600.00. The actual net VAT liability for the year ended 31 December 20X1 is £3,820.00.

1   When must Jump Ltd's VAT return be filed?

    A   31 January 20X2

    B   28 February 20X2

    C   31 March 20X2

2   Which ONE of the following statements about Jump Ltd's payment of VAT during the year ended 31 December 20X1 is true?

    A   Jump Ltd must make nine monthly payments of £360.00

    B   Jump Ltd must make nine monthly payments of £382.00

    C   Jump Ltd must make twelve monthly payments of £300.00

    D   Jump Ltd must make twelve monthly payments of £318.33

3   What is the balancing payment/repayment due from/to Jump Ltd when their VAT return for the year ended 31 December 20X1 is filed?

The annual accounting scheme can be used with the cash accounting scheme or with the flat rate scheme, but not both schemes.

Test your understanding 3

A VAT-registered business has a year end of 30 June 20X2 and uses the annual accounting scheme.

1   Which one of the following statements is true?

    A   The whole VAT liability for the year is payable on 30 June 20X2

    B   The whole VAT liability for the year is payable on 31 August 20X2

    C   The VAT liability is payable in nine monthly instalments starting on 31 October 20X1 with a balancing payment on 31 July 20X2

    D   The VAT liability is payable in nine monthly instalments starting on 31 October 20X1 with a balancing payment on 31 August 20X2

2   The annual VAT return is due to be submitted by which date?

    A   31 July 20X2

    B   31 August 20X2

 Reference material

Information about annual accounting is included in the indirect tax reference material provided in the real assessment, so you do not need to learn it.

It can be found in the 'Special accounting schemes' section.

You need to be familiar with the location and content of the material as in the assessment you will need to access the correct part of the reference material from a series of clickable links.

Why not look up the correct part of the indirect tax reference material in the appendix to this text book now?

3 Cash accounting

3.1 How the scheme works

Normally VAT is accounted for on the basis of invoices issued and received in a return period. Accordingly:

- Output VAT is paid to HMRC by reference to the period in which the tax point occurs (usually the delivery or invoice date), regardless of whether payment has been received from the customer.

- Input VAT is reclaimed from HMRC by reference to the invoices received in the return period, even if payment has not been made to the supplier.

However, under the cash accounting scheme a business accounts for VAT on the basis of when payment is actually received from customers or made to suppliers. The tax point becomes the date of receipt or payment.

Under the cash accounting scheme invoices will still be sent to customers and received from suppliers in the normal way, but the key record that must be kept is a cash book. This should summarise all the payments made and received and have a **separate column for VAT**.

3.2 Conditions

As with annual accounting, the scheme is aimed at smaller businesses, is optional to join and conditions need to be satisfied to be eligible to join.

- The trader's VAT returns must be up-to-date and they must have no convictions for VAT offences or penalties for dishonest conduct.

- Estimated taxable turnover, excluding VAT and sales of capital assets, must not exceed £1,350,000 for the next year.

- Once in the scheme, a trader must leave once their annual taxable turnover, excluding VAT, exceeds £1,600,000.

  If a business takes over another business as a going concern, the estimated taxable turnover (excluding VAT) of the new combined business must be assessed and compared to the £1,600,000 threshold to decide whether the business should immediately leave the scheme.

- When a business leaves the scheme they must account for all outstanding VAT (i.e. on amounts receivable less amounts payable), as they will be moving to a system where VAT is accounted for on invoices not on a cash basis.

3.3 Advantages and disadvantages

Advantages	Disadvantages
• Businesses selling on credit do not have to pay output VAT to HMRC until they receive cash from customers.	• Input tax cannot be claimed until the invoice is paid. This delays recovery of input VAT.
• This gives automatic relief for bad debts (i.e. irrecoverable debts) because if the customer does not pay, then the VAT on their invoice does not have to be paid over to HMRC. Cash flow is improved.	• Not suitable for businesses with a lot of cash sales or zero-rated supplies. • Using cash accounting in these situations just causes a delay in the recovery of input VAT.
• Cash accounting can be used together with annual accounting (but not the flat rate scheme).	• If a business uses cash accounting as soon as it registers, it will be unable to reclaim VAT on their stock (i.e. inventory) and assets until the invoices for these items are paid.

Test your understanding 4

Would each of the following businesses benefit from joining the cash accounting scheme? Select Yes or No for each business.

1   JB Ltd which operates a retail shop selling directly to the public. All sales are for cash and all purchases are made on credit. JB Ltd's supplies are all standard-rated.   YES/NO

2   Amber and Co, which manufactures and sells computer printers to other businesses. This is a standard-rated business and all sales and purchases are made on credit.   YES/NO

3   John Smith, a sole trader who manufactures children's shoes and sells them to retailers. This is a zero-rated activity and all sales and purchases are made on credit.   YES/NO

Test your understanding 5

Indicate whether the following statements about the cash accounting scheme are true or false.

Tick one box on each line.

		True	False
1	VAT invoices are not issued to customers		
2	The scheme gives automatic bad debt relief		
3	Cash accounting is useful for businesses with a high proportion of cash sales		
4	If a business adopts cash accounting then their customers cannot reclaim input VAT until they pay their invoices		
5	A business cannot join the cash accounting scheme if their VAT returns are not up-to-date		

Reference material

Information about cash accounting is included in the indirect tax reference material provided in the real assessment, so you do not need to learn it.

It can be found in the 'Special accounting schemes' section.

You need to be familiar with the location and content of the material as in the assessment you will need to access the correct part of the reference material from a series of clickable links.

Why not look up the correct part of the indirect tax reference material in the appendix to this text book now?

4 The flat rate scheme

4.1 Purpose of the scheme

The aim of the flat rate scheme is to simplify the way in which very small businesses calculate their VAT liability.

4.2 How the scheme works

Under the flat rate scheme, a business calculates its VAT liability by simply **applying a flat rate percentage to total VAT-inclusive turnover**.

This removes the need to calculate and record detailed output and input VAT information. In some cases it can save the business money.

- The flat rate percentage is applied to the gross (VAT-inclusive) **total turnover** figure.

  This includes standard-rated, zero-rated and exempt supplies.

  No input VAT is recovered.

- The percentage varies according to the type of trade in which the business is involved.

  In the first year in which a business is registered for VAT it will receive a 1% discount on its normal percentage.

  Note that if you need to use an appropriate percentage in the assessment it will be given to you.

- The flat rate scheme is **only** used to calculate the VAT due to HMRC.

  In other respects, VAT is dealt with in the normal way:

  – A **VAT invoice** must still be issued to customers and VAT charged at the appropriate rate.

  – A **VAT account** must still be maintained.

- The flat rate scheme can be used together with the annual accounting scheme.

- It is not possible to join both the flat rate scheme and the cash accounting scheme, however it is possible to request that the flat rate scheme calculations are performed on a cash paid/receipts basis.

4.3 Conditions for the scheme

The scheme is optional. However, in order to join the scheme, the **taxable** turnover of the business (excluding VAT), for the next 12 months, must not be expected to exceed £150,000.

Once in the scheme, a business can stay in until their **total VAT-inclusive** income (i.e. all turnover **including taxable and exempt supplies**) for the previous 12 months exceeds £230,000.

If a business takes over another business as a going concern, the total VAT-inclusive turnover (taxable and exempt) of the new combined business for the previous 12 months must be assessed and compared to the £230,000 threshold to decide whether the business should leave the scheme.

 Example

Simon runs a business selling computer supplies. He registered for VAT and joined the flat rate scheme a few years ago.

If the flat rate percentage for this type of business is 12%, how much VAT should Simon pay over for the quarter ended 30 June 20X0 when his turnover (including VAT) is £39,000?

Solution

£4,680.00 (£39,000 × 12%)

4.4 Advantages and disadvantages of the flat rate scheme

The advantages of the scheme include the following:

- A business does not have to record the VAT charged on each individual sale and purchase.

- Easier administration as the business does not have to decide which amounts of input VAT can be reclaimed and which cannot.

- The business gets a discount of 1% in the first year of registration.

- The business may pay less VAT than using the normal method.

- The business has certainty as the percentage of turnover that has to be paid over as VAT is known in advance.

- There is less chance of making a mistake in calculating VAT.

The percentage used in flat rate accounting is fixed for particular trade sectors and takes into account the mix of standard-rated, zero-rated and exempt sales made by the average business in that sector.

The scheme may not be suitable for businesses which do not have the same mix as an average business.

In particular it would not be suitable for:

- businesses that regularly receive repayments under normal VAT accounting

- businesses that buy a higher proportion of standard-rated items than others in their trade sector as they would not be able to reclaim the input VAT on these purchases

- businesses that make a higher proportion of zero-rated or exempt sales than others in their trade.

4.5 Limited cost businesses

If a business qualifies as a limited cost business then VAT will be calculated under the flat rate scheme using 16.5% rather than the percentage based on the business.

This removes one of the main advantages of the flat rate scheme and some businesses may actually pay more VAT than they would under the standard VAT system.

A business is classed as a limited cost business if its VAT inclusive expenditure on goods is less than either:

- 2% of its VAT inclusive turnover

- £1,000 a year (if its costs are more than 2% of VAT inclusive turnover).

Goods, for the purposes of the above, must be used exclusively for business purposes and exclude the following:

- capital expenditure

- food or drink for consumption by the flat rate business or its employees

- vehicles, vehicle parts and fuel (except where the business provides transport services- for example a taxi business).

Example

Claire runs a wedding photography business and uses the flat rate scheme to prepare her VAT returns.

Claire's VAT inclusive turnover for the quarter ended 30 September is £14,400. Her VAT inclusive cost of goods for this period was £900.

If the flat rate percentage for this type of business is 11%, how much VAT should Claire pay over for the quarter ended 30 September?

Solution

Claire's business is a limited cost business because her cost of goods is less than £1,000 (as this is greater than 2% of VAT inclusive turnover).

As a result her VAT should be calculated using a percentage of 16.5% rather than the relevant percentage for her business type.

£2,376 (£14,400 × 16.5%)

4.6 Reclaiming VAT on capital expenditure

If a business that qualifies for the flat rate scheme spends in excess of £2,000 on a capital item (VAT Inclusive) then the business can specifically recover the input VAT and this falls outside the flat rate system. This is referred to in the reference material.

In addition the input VAT needs to be recovered by adding it to box 4 of the VAT return (see chapter 7.)

Test your understanding 6

In the year ended 31 December 20X0, Apple Ltd has annual sales to the general public of £100,000, all of which are standard-rated.

The company incurs standard-rated expenses of £4,500 per annum.

These figures include VAT.

1   What is Apple Ltd's VAT liability using the normal method?

    A   £19,100.00

    B   £15,916.66

    C   £20,000.00

    D   £16,666.66

2   What is Apple Ltd's VAT liability using the flat rate method assuming a percentage of 9%?

    A   £20,000.00

    B   £16,666.66

    C   £9,000.00

    D   £8,595.00

Test your understanding 7

Indicate whether the following statements about the flat rate scheme are true or false.

Tick one box on each line.

		True	False
1	VAT invoices are not issued to customers.		
2	A VAT account need not be kept.		
3	Traders using the flat rate scheme can also join the annual accounting scheme.		
4	Traders can join the flat rate scheme if their taxable turnover for the last 12 months is below £230,000.		
5	The flat rate scheme percentage varies according to the trade sector of the business.		

 Test your understanding 8

Which one of the following is not an advantage of the flat rate scheme?

A   The business gets a discount of 1% on the flat rate percentage in the first year of registration

B   VAT returns do not need to be completed

C   The business does not have to record the VAT charged on individual sales and purchases

D   The business has easier administration as it does not have to decide which input VAT can be reclaimed and which cannot

Test your understanding 9

In the year ended 31 December 20X1, Pear Ltd has annual sales of £87,000, all of which are standard-rated and to the general public.

The company incurs standard-rated expenses of £6,100 per annum.

These figures are VAT-exclusive.

1   Select which of the following gives Pear Ltd's liability using the normal method.

   A   £13,483.33

   B   £17,400.00

   C   £16,180.00

   D   £14,500.00

2   Select which of the following gives Pear Ltd's VAT liability using the flat rate method assuming a percentage of 8%.

   A   £6,960.00

   B   £8,352.00

 Reference material

Information about the flat rate scheme is included in the indirect tax reference material provided in the real assessment, so you do not need to learn it.

It can be found in the 'Special accounting schemes' section.

You need to be familiar with the location and content of the material as in the assessment you will need to access the correct part of the reference material from a series of clickable links.

Why not look up the correct part of the indirect tax reference material in the appendix to this text book now?

5 Test your understanding

Test your understanding 10

1 Which one of the following statements is true?

A Traders using the normal accounting scheme usually submit their VAT returns every quarter

B Electronic VAT returns must be submitted 7 days after the end of the return period

C A trader is always permitted to pay VAT by sending a cheque through the post

2 What is the annual turnover threshold for eligibility to join the annual accounting scheme?

A £1,350,000

B £1,600,000

3 Is the following statement true or false?

The cash accounting scheme can be used at the same time as the annual accounting scheme   TRUE/FALSE

4 John's VAT liability for the previous year was £7,200.00. He estimates it will be £7,800.00 this year. He joins the annual accounting scheme.

What is the size of each instalment?

A £720.00

B £780.00

C £800.00

D £866.66

5 Which one of the following statements about cash accounting is false?

A Cash accounting is a disadvantage for a business selling zero-rated supplies

B VAT invoices need not be sent out

C The key record for determining VAT due is the cash book

6   Zak is a registered trader using the flat rate scheme with a percentage of 12%. His sales for the quarter are all standard-rated and are £75,000 inclusive of VAT. His business is not a limited cost business.

What VAT should he pay to HMRC for the quarter?

A   £9,000.00

B   £7,500.00

7   Trystan owns a business with an annual taxable turnover of £800,000 and uses the annual accounting scheme.

He transfers the business as a going concern to William and Sons which has an existing taxable turnover of £900,000 and also uses the annual accounting scheme.

Trystan is employed by William and Sons as the manager to run his former business.

Which of the following statements is true?

A   Trystan's part of the business can continue to use the annual accounting scheme until its turnover exceeds £1,600,000.

B   Trystan's part of the business can continue to use the annual accounting scheme for the next 12 months.

C   As the turnover of the combined business exceeds £1,600,000 the whole combined business is no longer eligible to be in the annual accounting scheme.

6 Summary

Clearly it is important for a business to know when they have to complete VAT returns and pay over VAT. The normal pattern is to complete returns and pay over VAT quarterly or monthly. This is the case unless the business has chosen annual accounting which is one of the special schemes aimed at smaller businesses.

Annual accounting gives the advantages of only one annual VAT return and fixed regular VAT payments. The turnover thresholds for the scheme are the same as for cash accounting.

Cash accounting changes the normal tax point rules and allows the business to pay VAT to HMRC when they actually receive the cash from their customers rather than the delivery or invoice date. This gives automatic relief for bad debts (i.e. irrecoverable debts) but has the disadvantage that input VAT can only be claimed when suppliers are paid.

The flat rate scheme is aimed at simplifying VAT accounting for the very small business. The amount of VAT payable is determined by simply applying a fixed percentage to the VAT-inclusive turnover of the business. However it is important to remember that the business still has to comply with the rules about issuing tax invoices.

Test your understanding answers

Test your understanding 1

1   The correct answer is C.

    31 October – one month after the end of the quarter.

2   The correct answer is D.

    7 November – 7 extra days are given for online submissions.

3   The correct answer is C.

    Direct debit payments are taken from the trader's bank account 3 working days after the extra 7 day period.

Test your understanding 2

1   The correct answer is B.

    28 February 20X2 = 2 months after the year end.

2   The correct answer is A.

    Nine monthly payments must be made, each of which are 10% of the VAT liability for the previous year.

3   The balancing payment will be £580.00

    (£3,820.00 – (£360.00 × 9))

Test your understanding 3

1   The correct answer is D.

    This is how the annual accounting scheme payments are made.

2   The correct answer is B.

    31 August 20X2 – two months after the year end.

Test your understanding 4

1 NO. As sales are all in cash, the adoption of the cash accounting scheme would not affect the time when output tax would be accounted for.

However, the recovery of input tax would be delayed until the business had paid its suppliers.

2 YES. The business would benefit because it would only account for output VAT when the customer paid.

Even though the recovery of input VAT would be delayed until the suppliers were paid, the amount of input VAT is likely to be less than output VAT so the business does gain a net cash flow advantage.

3 NO. As the sales are zero-rated no output tax is payable.
The adoption of the cash accounting scheme would simply delay the recovery of input VAT until the suppliers were paid.

 Test your understanding 5

1 False – VAT invoices must still be issued.

2 True – this is one of the advantages of the scheme.

3 False – businesses with a high level of cash sales do not benefit from cash accounting.

4 False – cash accounting does not affect customers.

5 True – this is one of the conditions for joining the scheme.

 Test your understanding 6

1 The correct answer is B.

£15,916.66 (20/120 × (£100,000 – £4,500))

2 The correct answer is C.

£9,000.00 (9% × £100,000)

Test your understanding 7

1   False – VAT invoices must still be supplied to customers.

2   False – A VAT account must still be kept.

3   True – It is possible to be in the flat rate and the annual accounting scheme.

4   False – the threshold to join the scheme is £150,000.

5   True – The flat rate percentage is determined by your trade sector.

 Test your understanding 8

The correct answer is B.

VAT returns must still be completed.

 Test your understanding 9

1   The correct answer is C.

(£87,000 – £6,100) × 20% = £16,180.00

2   The correct answer is B.

(£87,000 + 20% of £87,000) × 8% = £8,352.00

The percentage must be applied to the VAT-inclusive figure.

Test your understanding 10

1   The correct answer is A.

    B is false as the time limit is 1 month and 7 days after the end of the return period.

    C is false as traders cannot pay by post if they submit electronic returns.

2   The correct answer is A.

3   The statement is true.

4   The correct answer is A. (£7,200 ÷ 10) = £720.00

5   The correct answer is B.

6   The correct answer is A. (£75,000 × 12%) = £9,000.00.

7   The correct answer is C.

VAT errors and penalties

Introduction

This chapter is a short one explaining what happens if a business does not abide by all the VAT regulations.

Correction of errors is also covered. This is an important topic and will often be tested in the assessment task dealing with the actual completion of a VAT return.

ASSESSMENT CRITERIA	CONTENTS
Make adjustments and declarations for any errors or omissions identified in previous VAT periods (2.4)	1 Tax avoidance and evasion 2 Penalties 3 Default surcharge
Explain the implications for a business of failure to comply with registration requirements (3.1)	
Explain the implications for a business of failure to comply with the requirement to submit VAT returns (3.2)	
Explain the implications for a business of failure to comply with the requirement to make payment of VAT (3.3)	
Explain the implications for a business resulting from a failure to make error corrections in the proper manner or report errors where required to do so (3.4)	

1 Tax avoidance and evasion

1.1 Tax avoidance

Tax avoidance means arranging your tax affairs, using legal methods, so that you pay less tax.

For example, individuals and businesses can reduce their tax bills by claiming all the reliefs and allowances to which they are entitled. Sometimes a transaction can be timed to give maximum tax advantage.

Tax avoidance is legal.

1.2 Tax evasion

Tax evasion, however, is a criminal offence.

Tax evasion means using illegal methods to reduce tax due.

Typically this might be through concealing a source of income, deliberately understating income or over-claiming expenses and reliefs.

VAT could be evaded by under-declaring or concealing outputs and output tax or by overstating inputs and hence over-claiming input tax.

Although VAT evasion is a criminal offence, in many cases HMRC prefer to claim penalties and interest rather than pursue cases through the courts.

1.3 Ethical implications

AAT members and students are required to follow the AAT Code of Professional Ethics. These require that AAT members act with:

- integrity
- objectivity
- professional competence and due care
- confidentiality
- professional behaviour.

It is important for AAT members to ensure that information provided to HMRC is accurate and complete.

Members must not assist a client to plan or commit an offence. They should comply with relevant laws and avoid actions that may discredit the profession.

Any deliberate attempt to evade tax would be a breach of integrity and professional behaviour.

For example, if the dates on some invoices were deliberately altered so that they appeared in the next quarter's VAT return rather than the current one, then this would be a breach both of VAT regulations and the AAT Professional Code of Ethics.

In your assessment you may be presented with scenarios and alternative courses of action where you have to choose a suitable action which adheres to both the VAT regulations and the AAT's ethical code.

2 Penalties

2.1 Introduction

VAT has many regulations with which a business must comply.

As mentioned in Chapter 1, HMRC have powers to check whether a business is keeping to the rules.

- HMRC make occasional control visits to check that returns are correct.

- HMRC have the power to enter business premises and inspect records and documents.

If a business fails to comply with VAT regulations they will usually receive a penalty (fine).

The amount of the penalty varies according to the offence, but in recent years HMRC has been working to produce a standard penalty system.

For your assessment, you need to know the main principles of the enforcement regime but not the fine detail.

2.2 Summary of main penalties

Offence	Penalty
Failure to register	Standard penalty plus all VAT due from date registration should have taken place
Incorrect return (where error is careless or deliberate)	Standard penalty plus error must be corrected
Late returns and/or late payment	Default surcharge

2.3 Failure to register

Registration rules were dealt with in Chapter 2.

If a business fails to register when it should, then HMRC can issue an assessment asking them to pay over all the VAT due since the date it should have registered, plus a penalty can be levied.

The penalty is determined by the standard penalty regime which applies across all taxes and is a percentage of the VAT outstanding.

The percentage to use varies from 0% for genuine mistakes up to 100% for deliberate and concealed actions. The penalty can be reduced if the trader cooperates with HMRC.

2.4 Incorrect return

If a trader makes an error in a VAT return which leads to net VAT payable being understated this must be corrected (see below).

A net VAT error is calculated as the difference between the additional VAT due to HMRC less any VAT claimable by the trader.

Note that the amount of any errors or omissions will be given in the assessment.

A penalty may be charged if the error is careless or deliberate.

If a trader discovers a non-careless error, such as a simple mistake, then they must take steps to correct it. If they do not then HMRC will treat it as a careless error and a penalty may be charged.

If a trader does not submit a return at all then HMRC can issue an assessment which estimates the amount of VAT due. If this estimate is too low and a trader does not tell HMRC within 30 days that it is too low, then a penalty can be charged.

 Example

Bishop is a registered trader who prepares VAT returns quarterly. He discovers that in his previous quarter he entered VAT output tax on his return as £56,792.00 when it should have been £65,972.00. He also entered input tax as £45,510.00 when it should have been £45,150.00.

He also discovers that he has not reclaimed the VAT of £3,450.00 on the purchase of a new milling machine.

What is the net VAT error?

Solution

	£
Output tax understated (£65,972.00 – £56,792.00)	9,180.00
Input tax overstated (£45,510.00 – £45,150.00)	360.00
Input tax understated – not claimed on machine	(3,450.00)
Net VAT error (extra VAT due)	6,090.00

A penalty under the standard penalty regime may be charged.

This will be a percentage of the net VAT understated, and it varies from 0% to 100% of the error.

In addition, interest may be charged.

Reference material

Some information on penalties is included in the indirect tax reference material provided in the real assessment, so you do not need to learn it.

It can be found in the 'Surcharges, penalties and assessments' section.

You need to be familiar with the location and content of the material as in the assessment you will need to access the correct part of the reference material from a series of clickable links.

Why not look up the correct part of the indirect tax reference material in the appendix to this text book now?

2.5 Correcting errors – voluntary disclosure

If a trader discovers that they have made an error in an earlier VAT return then they must try to correct it as soon as possible.

There are two methods of correction depending on the size of error:

- include on next VAT return

   (only if non-deliberate and below threshold – see below)

- include on Form VAT 652 (Notification of Errors in VAT Returns)

   (or by letter if no form available).

The information that should be provided to the relevant HMRC VAT Error Correction Team (if the error is not corrected on the next return) is:

- how the error happened

- the amount of the error

- the VAT period in which it occurred

- whether the error was involving input or output tax

- how you worked out the error

- whether the error is in favour of the business or HMRC.

Note that a taxpayer must use Form VAT 652 (or a letter) for larger errors and where there is a deliberate error, but they may also use the form for smaller errors if desired. Taxpayers can even do both as there is a box on the form that indicates whether the error has been corrected on the return.

Form VAT 652 can be downloaded from the HMRC website.

The distinction between a small or large error is determined by the 'error correction reporting threshold'.

The following table explains the threshold limits and summarises which errors can be corrected on the next return and which must be separately disclosed.

Include on next VAT return	Submit on form 652
Errors may be corrected on the next VAT return if they are non-deliberate and: - no more than £10,000; or - between £10,000 and £50,000 but no more than 1% of turnover for the current return period (specifically the figure included in Box 6 of the VAT return – see Chapter 7).	Errors must be separately disclosed if they: - exceed £50,000; or - exceed £10,000 and are more than 1% of the turnover for the current return period (figure in Box 6 of the return); or - are a deliberate error; or - relate to an accounting period that ended > 4 years ago.

Reference material

Error limit information is included in the indirect tax reference material provided in the real assessment, so you do not need to learn it.

It can be found in the 'Errors in previous VAT returns' section.

You need to be familiar with the location and content of the material as in the assessment you will need to access the correct part of the reference material from a series of clickable links.

Why not look up the correct part of the indirect tax reference material in the appendix to this text book now?

 Test your understanding 1

You are given the following information about the net errors and turnover of four businesses.

For each of them, indicate whether they can correct the error on the next VAT return or whether separate disclosure is required.

Tick ONE box on EACH line.

Assume none of the errors are deliberate and relate to recent accounting periods.

Net error £ p	Turnover £	Include in VAT return	Separate disclosure
4,500.00	100,000		
12,000.00	250,000		
30,000.00	3,500,000		
60,000.00	10,000,000		

Test your understanding 2

You are given the following information about the non-deliberate net errors and turnover of four businesses.

For each of them, indicate whether they can correct the error on the next VAT return or whether separate disclosure is required.

Tick ONE box on EACH line.

Net error £	Turnover £	Include in VAT return	Separate disclosure
40,000	4,500,000		
55,000	6,000,000		
12,500	300,000		
4,500	40,000		

2.6 Errors found by HMRC

An error may be discovered by HMRC, for example during a VAT control visit. In this case HMRC may issue a discovery assessment (i.e. a demand) to collect any VAT due.

Normally HMRC have up to 4 years after the end of the return period in which the error occurred to issue an assessment.

This is extended to 20 years for deliberate behaviour (such as fraud).

HMRC can also issue a penalty under the standard penalty regime and charge interest on the unpaid VAT.

Any penalty is likely to be higher than if the trader found the error themselves and voluntarily disclosed it.

2.7 Failure to disclose business changes

Changes to the registration details of a business must be notified to HMRC within 30 days. Otherwise a penalty may be charged.

For example, changes that must be notified include changes in address, type of supplies made, and type of business (e.g. change from sole trader to partnership).

A penalty is unlikely to be charged if there is no loss of VAT to HMRC.

2.8 VAT penalty in fraud cases

A new penalty has been introduced for participation in VAT fraud.

If a business knew or should have known that their transactions were connected to a VAT fraud there is a fixed liability of 30% of potential lost revenue. This is in addition to denying the business recovery of the input VAT associated with the transactions.

2.9 Summary of errors and omissions

Error/omissions	Action
Failing to register	HMRC can issue assessment to collect tax due and charge a penalty.
Failure to submit a return	HMRC can issue an assessment to collect tax due.
Failure to tell HMRC that an assessment is too low within 30 days	Penalty can be charged.
Making a non-careless error	Must take steps to correct otherwise error may be regarded as careless.
Making a careless or deliberate error	Trader must correct the error. HMRC can charge a penalty.
Correcting errors	Inclusion on Form VAT 652 or by letter. If below limit can include on next return.
Errors found by HMRC	HMRC can raise an assessment within 4 years of the end of the VAT period (careless errors) or 20 years (deliberate errors like fraud). A penalty can be charged.
Submitting VAT return late or paying late	Default surcharge regime applies.
Failure to disclose business changes	Penalty can be charged.
Participation in VAT fraud	Fixed penalty can be charged as well as denying recovery of associated input VAT.

> ### 📋 Reference material
>
> Much of this information is included in the indirect tax reference material provided in the real assessment, so you do not need to learn it.
>
> It can be found in the 'Errors in previous VAT returns' and 'Surcharges, penalties and assessments' section.
>
> You need to be familiar with the location and content of the material as in the assessment you will need to access the correct part of the reference material from a series of clickable links.
>
> Why not look up the correct part of the indirect tax reference material in the appendix to this text book now?

3 Default surcharge

3.1 Surcharge liability notice

If a trader commits a **default** by submitting their VAT return late or paying their VAT late, HMRC will serve a **surcharge liability notice**.

This identifies a surcharge period which runs until 12 months after the end of the period for which the trader is in default.

> ### 💡 Example
>
> Jolene submits her return for the quarter ended 30 June 20X6 on 15 August 20X6 but pays her VAT electronically on 3 August 20X6.
>
> As this is a late return, a surcharge liability notice will be issued by HMRC which will cover the period up to 30 June 20X7.

3.2 Effect of surcharge liability notice

The surcharge liability notice acts as a warning to the trader.

If they commit a further default within the surcharge period then:

(i) the surcharge period is extended so it now ends 12 months after the end of the new default period, and

(ii) if the default is a late VAT payment (rather than just a late VAT return), then the trader is charged a **surcharge** penalty which is a fixed percentage of the VAT overdue.

The process is repeated if the trader commits further defaults within the surcharge period, with increasing levels of penalty charged.

Hence the trader needs to stay free of defaults for twelve months to come out of the default surcharge system.

For assessment purposes you are not expected to know how the amount of the surcharge is calculated.

Reference material

Some information on surcharges is included in the indirect tax reference material provided in the real assessment, so you do not need to learn it.

It can be found in the 'Surcharges, penalties and assessments' section.

You need to be familiar with the location and content of the material as in the assessment you will need to access the correct part of the reference material from a series of clickable links.

Why not look up the correct part of the indirect tax reference material in the appendix to this text book now?

3.3 Reasonable excuse

A surcharge liability notice will not be issued if the trader has a **reasonable excuse** for submitting their return or paying their VAT late.

Examples of reasonable excuse include:

- computer breakdown just before or during the preparation of the return or loss of records due to fire or flood

- illness of an employee who prepares the return where no one else can do the work

- sudden cash crisis such as loss of cash due to theft or major customer becoming insolvent.

Note that a lack of funds to pay the tax is not considered to be a reasonable excuse.

4 Test your understanding

 Test your understanding 3

1   Tax avoidance is illegal and tax evasion is legal.

    True or False?

2   Which one of the following is a consequence of submitting an incorrect VAT return?

    A   A penalty may be charged and the error must be corrected on the next VAT return

    B   A penalty may be charged and the error must be corrected by submitting it on Form VAT 652

    C   A penalty will be charged and the way in which the error is corrected depends on its size

    D   A penalty may be charged and the way in which the error is corrected depends on its size

3   Tariq finds that he made a non-deliberate net error on an earlier VAT return of £12,400.00. If his turnover for the current quarter is £750,000 how should he correct the error?

    A   By inclusion on his next VAT return

    B   By separate notification on Form VAT 652 or by letter

4   Fill in the blanks in the following statements.

    A surcharge liability notice runs for .... months after the end of the return period for which the trader is in default.

    Once the surcharge period has started a VAT default occurs when VAT is paid .....

    A surcharge liability notice will not be issued if a trader has a .... excuse.

Test your understanding 4

Indicate whether the following statements about VAT errors and penalties are true or false.

Tick one box on each line

		True	False
1	If a trader fails to register at the correct time they will have to pay over all the VAT they should have charged to customers since the date they should have been registered.		
2	If a trader makes an error in a VAT return they will always be charged a penalty.		
3	A default only occurs if a trader both pays VAT late and submits a VAT return late.		
4	Surcharge liability notices cover a period of 12 months.		

5 Summary

It is important to know the difference between tax avoidance and evasion as the former is legal and the latter is not.

VAT is a self-assessed tax – that is traders calculate their own VAT liability. HMRC have powers to visit businesses and check that they are complying with the rules. If not, penalties can be charged.

For your assessment you need to know the main principles of the enforcement regime, but not the fine detail.

The three main penalties examinable are: late registration, incorrect returns and late submission of VAT returns and payments.

Late registration and errors in returns are dealt with under the common penalty regime. The penalty is not a fixed monetary amount but is determined as a percentage of VAT outstanding. The percentage varies according to the trader's actions and level of cooperation.

The default surcharge applies to late returns and payments. The chief assessor has stated that you need to know what triggers a surcharge liability notice but you will not be expected to know how the amount of the surcharge is calculated.

Correction of errors is an important area. You may be asked to deal with the correction of errors in the assessment task on completion of the VAT return.

Test your understanding answers

Test your understanding 1

1   Error £4,500.00 – include on VAT return as below £10,000

2   Error £12,000.00 – separate disclosure is needed as this error is more than £10,000 and is more than 1% of turnover

3   Error £30,000.00 – can be included on VAT return as between £10,000 and £50,000 and less than 1% of turnover

4   Error £60,000.00 – must be separately disclosed as more than £50,000

Test your understanding 2

1   Include in VAT return.

    The error is between £10,000 and £50,000 and less than 1% of turnover.

2   Separate disclosure. The error is more than £50,000.

3   Separate disclosure.

    The error is over £10,000 and more than 1% of turnover.

4   Include in VAT return. The error is less than £10,000.

Test your understanding 3

1   False – it is the other way round. Avoidance is legal and evasion is illegal.

2   The correct answer is D.

    Whether or not a penalty is charged depends on the circumstances.

3   The correct answer is B.

    The error is between £10,000 and £50,000 but is more than 1% of turnover, hence it must be separately disclosed.

4   A surcharge liability notice runs for …**12**.. months after the end of the return period for which the trader is in default.

    Once the surcharge period has started a VAT default occurs when VAT is paid …**late**.

    A surcharge liability notice will not be issued if a trader has a …**reasonable**…excuse.

 Test your understanding 4

1   True

2   False – whether or not a penalty is charged depends on the circumstances.

3   False – a default occurs when a return is submitted late OR a late payment made. It does not have to be both.

4   True

VAT returns

7

Introduction

In the final two chapters of this study text we are going to conclude our VAT studies by looking at how to complete a VAT return correctly and on time.

Businesses must complete a VAT return (a VAT 100 form) at the end of each quarter. The purpose of a VAT return is to summarise the transactions of a business for a period. In the assessment you will be required to complete an organisation's online VAT return.

ASSESSMENT CRITERIA
Identify and analyse relevant information on VAT (1.1)
Extract relevant data from the accounting records (2.1)
Calculate relevant input and output tax (2.2)
Calculate the VAT due to, or from, the relevant tax authority (2.3)
Make adjustments and declarations for any errors or omissions identified in previous VAT periods (2.4)
Complete and submit a VAT return and make any associated payment within statutory limits (2.5)
Inform the appropriate person about VAT-related matters (4.1)
Communicate information about VAT due to or from the tax authority (4.2)

CONTENTS

1 The VAT return
2 Completing the VAT return
3 Communicating VAT information

1 The VAT return

1.1 Introduction

The tax period for VAT is **three months**, or one month for taxpayers who choose to make monthly returns (normally taxpayers who receive regular refunds).

The taxpayer must complete a **VAT return at the end of each quarter**. The return summarises all the transactions for the period.

1.2 Timing of the VAT return

The taxpayer must submit the return within one month of the end of the tax period (paper) or 1 month and 7 days (electronic). The taxable person must ensure that the amount due (i.e. output tax collected less input tax deducted) clears HMRC bank account at the same time unless a direct debit payment arrangement exists.

For more detail on VAT returns and payments refer back to Chapter 5.

If a VAT repayment is due from HMRC the VAT return must still be completed and submitted to the same time deadlines as normal in order to be able to reclaim the amount due.

1.3 What a VAT return looks like

Virtually all businesses have to file their returns online rather than on paper.

In the assessment you will have to complete a VAT return which is likely to look as shown in section 1.4.

1.4 VAT return – online style

		£
VAT due in the period on **sales** and other outputs	**Box 1**	
VAT due in the period on **acquisitions** from other **EC Member States**	**Box 2**	
Total VAT due (**the sum of boxes 1 and 2**)	**Box 3**	
VAT reclaimed in the period on **purchases** and other inputs, including acquisitions from the EC	**Box 4**	
Net VAT to be paid to HM Revenue & Customs or reclaimed (**Difference between boxes 3 and 4**)	**Box 5**	
Total value of **sales** and all other outputs excluding any VAT. **Include your box 8 figure**	**Box 6**	
Total value of purchases and all other inputs excluding any VAT. **Include your box 9 figure**	**Box 7**	
Total value of all **supplies** of goods and related costs, excluding any VAT, to other **EC Member States**	**Box 8**	
Total value of all **acquisitions** of goods and related costs, excluding any VAT, from other **EC Member States**	**Box 9**	

As you can **see** there are nine boxes to complete with the relevant figures.

In reality, boxes 3 and 5, which are subtotals, are automatically filled in for an online return so you only have to complete seven boxes. When you practise completing the return you will have to fill these boxes in yourself.

Boxes 2, 8 and 9 are to do with supplies of goods and services to other European Union (EU) Member States and acquisitions from EU Member States. These will be considered in Chapter 8.

Note that the EU was formerly known as the EC (European Community) and the VAT returns on HMRC's website still use the previous name. However, either of these abbreviations (EU or EC) may be used by the chief assessor in the assessment.

2 Completing the VAT return

2.1 The VAT account

The main source of information for the VAT return is the VAT account.

The VAT account is a record which must be maintained by the trader to show the amount of VAT that is due to or from HMRC at the end of each quarter. It provides the link between the VAT return entries and the underlying business records.

It is important that the figures on the VAT return are extracted from the original business records, such as verified daybooks or journals.

Entries in these ledgers must be made with integrity and with knowledge of the requirements of VAT records and regulation of VAT administration.

The use of a company's audited accounting records will satisfy the integrity of the information.

If a statutory audit of the business is not required, it should nonetheless make its own internal checks to ensure that the information extracted from the records and taken to the VAT account is accurate and complete.

It is also important to realise that the balance on the VAT account should agree to the balance of VAT payable/reclaimable on the VAT return.

In the assessment you may be asked to select reasons why there is a difference between the balance on the VAT account and the balance per the VAT return.

Accordingly, it is important that you understand the purpose and content of both the VAT account and the VAT return.

2.2 How the VAT account should look

Given below is a pro-forma VAT account as suggested by the VAT Guide 19.14.

Numbers have been omitted for clarity.

1 January 20X5 to 31 March 20X5			
VAT deductible – input tax	£ p	**VAT payable – output tax**	£ p
VAT you have been charged on your purchases		VAT you have charged on your sales	
January	X	January	X
February	X	February	X
March	X	March	X
VAT allowable on acquisitions (Chapter 8)	X	VAT due on acquisitions	X
Adjustments of previous errors (if within the error limit – Chapter 6)			
Net input tax adjustments	X	Net output tax adjustments	X
Bad debt relief (section 2.6)	X		
Less: VAT on credits received from suppliers (e.g. credit notes received)	(X)	Less: VAT on credits allowed to customers (e.g. credit notes issued)	(X)
Total tax deductible	X	Total tax payable	X
		Less: Total tax deductible	(X)
		Payable to HMRC	X

The VAT account is part of the trader's double entry bookkeeping system.

However, the VAT on credit notes received in this example is deducted from input tax and the VAT on credit notes issued is deducted from output tax instead of being credited and debited respectively.

This is because this is how credit notes are dealt with in the VAT return.

However, businesses do not have to prepare their VAT account in exactly this way.

Reference material

Information about the contents of a VAT account is included in the indirect tax reference material provided in the real assessment, so you do not need to learn it.

It can be found in the 'Keeping business records and VAT records' section.

You need to be familiar with the location and content of the material as in the assessment you will need to access the correct part of the reference material from a series of clickable links.

Why not look up the correct part of the indirect tax reference material in the appendix to this text book now?

Test your understanding 1

Eagle runs a small business making only standard-rated supplies. The balance due to HMRC per her VAT account is £3,472.56.

She subsequently discovers the following errors:

1   She has recorded a credit note due to a customer of £81 including VAT, as a credit note from a supplier.

2   A purchase invoice of £420 including VAT has been omitted from the purchase day book.

After these corrections have been made, what is the corrected balance of VAT due to HMRC?

A   £3,389.06

B   £3,375.56

C   £3,429.56

D   £3,569.56

 Test your understanding 2

Lendl runs a small business making only standard-rated supplies.

The balance of VAT repayable by HMRC in Lendl's VAT account is £2,246.39. However, when he completes his VAT return it shows VAT repayable of only £1,976.75.

Lendl checks his figures and finds one error.

Which of the following is the error that explains the difference?

A   VAT recoverable on purchases is recorded as £5,140.62 in the VAT account but has been entered as £5,410.26 in the VAT return calculations

B   Lendl issued a credit note to a customer of £808.92 including VAT. The VAT has been correctly dealt with in the VAT account but in the VAT return workings it has been treated as a credit note from a supplier.

2.3 Information required for the VAT return

Boxes 1 to 4 of the VAT return can be fairly easily completed from the information in the VAT account. However, Boxes 6 and 7 require figures for total sales and purchases excluding VAT.

This information will need to be extracted from the original verified (preferably audited) ledger account totals posted up from the accounting records such as the sales day book and purchases day book totals. It is also possible that information relating to VAT could be shown in a journal.

Boxes 8 and 9 require figures, excluding VAT, for the value of supplies to other EU Member States and acquisitions from other EU Member States (dealt with in Chapter 8).

Therefore the accounting records should be designed in such a way that these figures can also be easily identified.

Reference material

Guidance on completing the VAT return is included in the indirect tax reference material provided in the real assessment, so you do not need to learn it.

It can be found in the 'Completing the VAT return, box by box' section.

You need to be familiar with the location and content of the material as in the assessment you will need to access the correct part of the reference material from a series of clickable links.

Why not look up the correct part of the indirect tax reference material in the appendix to this text book now?

Test your understanding 3

You are preparing the VAT return for Panther Alarms Ltd.

You must first complete the double entry for a few items to enable you to complete the VAT account and then extract the information you need to complete the VAT return.

Here is a list of possible sources of accounting information.

1   Sales day book

2   Sales returns day book

3   Bad and doubtful debts account (or impairment losses account)

4   Purchase returns day book

5   Drawings account

6   Purchases day book

7   Cash book

8   Assets account

9   Petty cash book

Enter the appropriate number from the list above against each item below to show the best sources of information for the figures required.

If you think the information will be in more than one place then give the number for both.

Figures required to complete the VAT return:

A   sales

B   cash sales

C   credit notes issued

D   purchases

E   cash purchases

F   credit notes received

G   capital goods sold

H   capital goods purchased

I   bad debt relief

 Example

Given below is a VAT account for Thompson Brothers for the second VAT quarter of 20X5.

Thompson Brothers Ltd
1 April 20X5 to 30 June 20X5

VAT deductible – input tax		VAT payable – output tax	
VAT on purchases	£	*VAT on sales*	£
April	700.00	April	1,350.00
May	350.00	May	1,750.00
June	350.00	June	700.00
	1,400.00		3,800.00
Other adjustments			
Less: Credit notes received	(20.00)	Less: Credit notes issued	(120.00)
Total tax deductible	1,380.00	Total tax payable	3,680.00
		Less: Total tax deductible	(1,380.00)
		Payable to HMRC	2,300.00

You are also given the summarised totals from the day books for the three-month period:

Sales day book

	Net £	VAT £	Total £
Standard-rated	19,000.00	3,800.00	22,800.00
Zero-rated	800.00	–	800.00

Sales returns day book

	Net £	VAT £	Total £
Standard-rated	600.00	120.00	720.00
Zero-rated	40.00	–	40.00

Purchases day book

	Net £	VAT £	Total £
Standard-rated	7,000.00	1,400.00	8,400.00
Zero-rated	2,000.00	–	2,000.00

Purchases returns day book

	Net £	VAT £	Total £
Standard-rated	100.00	20.00	120.00
Zero-rated	–	–	–

We are now in a position to complete the VAT return.

Solution

Step 1

Fill in Box 1 with the VAT on sales less the VAT on credit notes issued.

This can be taken either from the VAT account or from the day book summaries:
(£3,800 – £120) = £3,680.00.

Note that the figures in Boxes 1 – 5 you should include pence so put '.00' at the end if there are no pence in the total.

Step 2

Fill in Box 2 with the VAT payable on acquisitions from other EU Member states – none here.

Note that for Boxes 1 – 5, if there is no entry for a box, '0.00' should be put in the box.

Step 3

Complete Box 3 with the total of Boxes 1 and 2:
(£3,680.00 + £0.00) = £3,680.00.

Step 4

Fill in Box 4 with the total of VAT on all purchases less the total VAT on any credit notes received.

These figures can either be taken from the VAT account or from the day book totals:
(£1,400.00 – £20.00) = £1,380.00.

Step 5

Complete Box 5 by deducting the figure in Box 4 from the total in Box 3:
(£3,680.00 – £1,380.00) = £2,300.00.

This is the amount due to HMRC and should equal the balance on the VAT account.

If the Box 4 figure is larger than the Box 3 total then there is more input tax reclaimable than output tax to pay – this means that this is the amount being reclaimed from HMRC.

Step 6

Fill in Box 6 with the VAT-exclusive figure of all sales less credit notes issued.

In this example the information will come from the day books:
(£19,000 + £800 − £600 − £40) = £19,160

Note that this figure includes zero-rated supplies and any exempt supplies that are made.

Note that the figures in Boxes 6 − 9 should be whole pounds only. In the assessment it does not matter if the numbers are rounded up or down.

Step 7

Fill in Box 7 with the VAT-exclusive total of all purchases less credit notes received.

Again in this example this will be taken from the day books:
(£7,000 + £2,000 − £100) = £8,900

Step 8

Boxes 8 and 9 are for transactions with EU member states. These are dealt with in Chapter 8.

Note that for Boxes 6 − 9, if there is no entry for any box then '0' should be put in the box.

Step 9

If VAT is due to HMRC then payment must be made in accordance with the usual time limits. For assessment purposes you may be asked to state the payment date, or complete an email advising when this amount will be paid.

		£
VAT due in the period on **sales** and other outputs	Box 1	3,680.00
VAT due in the period on **acquisitions** from other **EU*** **Member States**	Box 2	0.00
Total VAT due (**the sum of boxes 1 and 2**)	Box 3	3,680.00
VAT reclaimed in the period on **purchases** and other inputs, including acquisitions from the **EU***	Box 4	1,380.00
Net VAT to be paid to HM Revenue & Customs or reclaimed (**Difference between boxes 3 and 4**)	Box 5	2,300.00
Total value of **sales** and all other outputs excluding any VAT. **Include your box 8 figure**	Box 6	19,160
Total value of purchases and all other inputs excluding any VAT. **Include your box 9 figure**	Box 7	8,900
Total value of all **supplies** of goods and related costs, excluding any VAT, to other **EU* Member States**	Box 8	0
Total value of all **acquisitions** of goods and related costs, excluding VAT, from other **EU* Member States**	Box 9	0

* In your assessment either EU or EC may be used in these boxes

If the business makes sales or purchases for cash then the relevant net and VAT figures from the cash receipts and payments books and petty cash book should also be included on the VAT return.

Note that in your assessment you are normally given extracts from ledger accounts rather than day book totals. However, you must understand how accounting information flows through from the books of original entry.

For this reason the Test your understanding questions include some where information is given in the form of ledger accounts and some where you are given daybook and cash book totals.

Test your understanding 4

Given below is the summary of relevant ledger accounts for a business for the three months ended 31 March 20X1.

Sales and sales returns account						
Date 20X1	Reference	Debit £	Date 20X1	Reference	Credit £	
1/1 to 31/03	SRDB Std-rated	1,625.77	1/1 to 31/03	SDB Std-rated	15,485.60	
1/1 to 31/03	SRDB Zero-rated	106.59	1/1 to 31/03	SDB Zero-rated	1,497.56	
31/03	Bal c/d	15,250.80				
	Total	16,983.16		Total	16,983.16	

Purchases and purchase returns account					
Date 20X1	Reference	Debit £	Date 20X1	Reference	Credit £
1/1 to 31/03	PDB Std-rated	8,127.45	1/1 to 31/03	PRDB Std-rated	935.47
1/1 to 31/03	PDB Zero-rated	980.57	1/1 to 31/03	PRDB Zero-rated	80.40
			31/03	Bal c/d	8,092.15
	Total	9,108.02		Total	9,108.02

VAT account					
Date 20X1	Reference	Debit £	Date 20X1	Reference	Credit £
31/03	PDB	1,625.49	31/03	SDB	3,097.12
31/03	SRDB	325.15	31/03	PRDB	187.09
	Bal c/d	1,333.57			
	Total	3,284.21		Total	3,284.21

Abbreviations key

SDB – sales day book, SDRB – sales returns day book
PDB – purchases day book, PRDB – purchase returns day book

Required

Prepare the VAT return for the quarter ended 31 March.

Pro-forma VAT return for completion

		£
VAT due in the period on **sales** and other outputs	**Box 1**	
VAT due in the period on **acquisitions** from other **EC Member States**	**Box 2**	
Total VAT due (**the sum of boxes 1 and 2**)	**Box 3**	
VAT reclaimed in the period on **purchases** and other inputs, including acquisitions from the EC	**Box 4**	
Net VAT to be paid to HM Revenue & Customs or reclaimed (**Difference between boxes 3 and 4**)	**Box 5**	
Total value of **sales** and all other outputs excluding any VAT. **Include your box 8 figure**	**Box 6**	
Total value of purchases and all other inputs excluding any VAT. **Include your box 9 figure**	**Box 7**	
Total value of all **supplies** of goods and related costs, excluding any VAT, to other **EC Member States**	**Box 8**	
Total value of all **acquisitions** of goods and related costs, excluding any VAT, from other **EC Member States**	**Box 9**	

2.4 VAT: Adjustment of previous errors

You will notice in the pro-forma VAT account that there are entries for net under claims and net over claims.

Net errors made in previous VAT returns which are below the disclosure threshold can be adjusted for on the VAT return through the VAT account.

The error threshold was discussed in Chapter 6.

As a reminder errors can be corrected on the next VAT return if they are non-deliberate and are:

- no more than £10,000

- between £10,000 and £50,000 but no more than 1% of turnover for the current return period (specifically the figure included in Box 6 of the return).

An error affecting output tax is adjusted by adding or subtracting it to Box 1. An error affecting input tax is adjusted for in Box 4.

If there are several errors they are netted off and the one single figure for net errors will then be entered as additional input tax in Box 4 if there has been an earlier net under claim of VAT and as additional output tax in Box 1 if the net error was a net over claim in a previous return.

To summarise:

	Box 1	Box 4
Single error affecting output tax	✓	
Single error affecting input tax		✓
Net errors resulting in VAT over claimed in past	✓	
Net errors resulting in VAT under claimed in past		✓

2.5 Errors above the threshold

For deliberate errors or errors above the 'error correction threshold', the HMRC VAT Error Correction Team should be informed immediately either by a letter or on Form VAT 652. This is known as voluntary disclosure.

The information that should be provided to the VAT office was included in Chapter 6.

Test your understanding 5

You are a self-employed accounting technician and Duncan Bye, a motor engineer, is one of your clients. He is registered for VAT.

His records for the quarter ended 30 June 20X1 showed the following:

Sales account					
Date 20X1	Reference	Debit £	Date 20X1	Reference	Credit £
			April	SDB	6,960.00
			May	SDB	6,510.00
			June	SDB	8,550.00
30/06	Bal c/d	22,020.00			
	Total	22,020.00		Total	22,020.00

Purchases account					
Date 20X1	Reference	Debit £	Date 20X1	Reference	Credit £
April	PDB	3,150.00			
May	PDB	3,270.00			
June	PDB	2,680.00			
			30/06	Bal c/d	9,100.00
	Total	9,100.00		Total	9,100.00

VAT account					
Date 20X1	Reference	Debit £	Date 20X1	Reference	Credit £
April	PDB	630.00	April	SDB	1,350.00
May	PDB	654.00	May	SDB	1,302.00
June	PDB	536.00	June	SDB	1,648.00
	Total			Total	

The VAT account has not yet been balanced off.

He also gives you some details of petty cash expenditure in the quarter which has not yet been entered into the ledger.

	£ p
Net purchases	75.60
VAT	15.12
	90.72

Duncan understated his output VAT by £24 on his last return. This is to be corrected on his current return.

Prepare the following VAT form 100 for the period.

		£
VAT due in the period on **sales** and other outputs	Box 1	
VAT due in the period on **acquisitions** from other **EU Member States**	Box 2	
Total VAT due (**the sum of boxes 1 and 2**)	Box 3	
VAT reclaimed in the period on **purchases** and other inputs, including acquisitions from the EU	Box 4	
Net VAT to be paid to HM Revenue & Customs or reclaimed (**Difference between boxes 3 and 4**)	Box 5	
Total value of **sales** and all other outputs excluding any VAT. **Include your box 8 figure**	Box 6	
Total value of purchases and all other inputs excluding any VAT. **Include your box 9 figure**	Box 7	
Total value of all **supplies** of goods and related costs, excluding any VAT, to other **EU Member States**	Box 8	
Total value of all **acquisitions** of goods and related costs, excluding any VAT, from other **EU Member States**	Box 9	

2.6   VAT: Bad debt relief

You will notice that there is an entry in the pro-forma VAT account for bad debt relief (also referred to as irrecoverable debt relief) as additional input tax.

When a supplier invoices a customer for an amount including VAT, the supplier must pay the VAT to HMRC.

If the customer then fails to pay the debt, the supplier's position is that he has paid output VAT which he has never collected.

This is obviously unfair, and the system allows him to recover such amounts.

Suppliers **cannot issue credit notes** to recover VAT on bad debts.

Instead, the business must make an **adjustment through the VAT return**. The business can reclaim VAT already paid over if:

- output tax was paid on the original supply

- six months have elapsed between the date payment was due (or the date of supply if later) and the date of the VAT return, and

- the debt has been written off as a bad debt in the accounting records

- the debt is between six months and 4 years and six months old

- the debt has not been sold to a factoring company

- the business did not charge more than the selling price for the items.

If the business receives a **repayment of the debt later**, it must make an adjustment to the VAT relief claimed.

The bad debt relief is entered in Box 4 of the return along with the VAT on purchases.

Be very careful when computing the VAT on the bad debt.

Check carefully to see if the amount of the bad debt given in the question is VAT-inclusive. This is likely because the amount the customer owes is the amount that includes VAT.

To calculate the VAT for a VAT-inclusive debt, you should multiply the bad debt by 20/120 (or 1/6) for standard-rated items.

On the cessation of a business, a claim can be made for relief on all outstanding debts up to the date of cessation.

It may be possible to claim bad debt relief for bad debts of a business bought by another business as a going concern, provided that the VAT registration of the target business is transferred to the acquiring business.

Example

A business has made purchases of £237,000 (net of VAT) in the VAT quarter and has written off a bad debt of £750 (including VAT).

They also have a net under claim of VAT of £1,250.00 from earlier periods.

Calculate the figure that will be entered on the VAT return for the quarter in Box 4.

Solution

	£	£ p
Purchases (net of VAT)	237,000	
VAT thereon (£237,000 × 20%)		47,400.00
Bad debt	750	
VAT thereon (£750 × 20/120)		125.00
Net under claim of VAT		1,250.00
		————
Total VAT for Box 4		48,775.00
		————

 Test your understanding 6

Jonas wrote off a bad debt on 3 June 20X6.

The goods had been delivered to the customer on 14 February 20X6 and the invoice was due for payment on 15 March 20X6.

Jonas does not use the cash accounting scheme.

What is the earliest that VAT can be claimed?

A   Quarter ending 31 May 20X6

B   Quarter ending 31 August 20X6

C   Quarter ending 30 November 20X6

D   Quarter ending 28 February 20X7

Reference material

Information on bad debt relief is included in the indirect tax reference material provided in the real assessment, so you do not need to learn it.

It can be found in the 'Bad debts' section.

You need to be familiar with the location and content of the material as in the assessment you will need to access the correct part of the reference material from a series of clickable links.

Why not look up the correct part of the indirect tax reference material in the appendix to this text book now?

2.7 Purchase of items with non-recoverable VAT

When a business spends money on UK customer entertaining and cars with some private use, they cannot recover input VAT. VAT on these items must not be included in the input VAT recoverable in Box 4 of the return.

If a business buys zero-rated items there will not be any VAT to include in Box 4.

There are different views on how the purchases of these items should be dealt with in Box 7 of the return. However, for this assessment the VAT-exclusive figure for all purchases, including zero-rated purchases and items on which VAT cannot be recovered, is included in Box 7.

Test your understanding 7

You are provided with the following summary of Mark Ambrose's books and other information provided by Mark for the quarter ended 30 September 20X1.

MARK AMBROSE

Summary of day books and petty cash expenditure
Quarter ended 30 September 20X1

Sales day book

	Work done £	VAT £	Total £
July	12,900.00	2,580.00	15,480.00
August	13,200.00	2,640.00	15,840.00
September	12,300.00	2,460.00	14,760.00
	38,400.00	7,680.00	46,080.00

Purchase day book

	Net £	VAT £	Total £
July	5,250.00	1,050.00	6,300.00
August	5,470.00	1,094.00	6,564.00
September	5,750.00	1,150.00	6,900.00
	16,470.00	3,294.00	19,764.00

On 30 September Mark purchased a car for £8,400 including VAT.

This car is to be used by Mark for business and private purposes.

The purchase of the car has not yet been recorded in the books.

Bad debts list – 30 September 20X1

Date debt due	Customer	Total (including VAT)
30 November 20X0	High Melton Farms	£300.00
3 January 20X1	Concorde Motors	£180.00
4 April 20X1	Bawtry Engineering	£120.00

These have now been written off as bad debts.

Complete boxes 1 to 9 of the VAT return for the quarter ended
30 September 20X1.

		£
VAT due in the period on **sales** and other outputs	**Box 1**	
VAT due in the period on **acquisitions** from other **EC Member States**	**Box 2**	
Total VAT due (**the sum of boxes 1 and 2**)	**Box 3**	
VAT reclaimed in the period on **purchases** and other inputs, including acquisitions from the EC	**Box 4**	
Net VAT to be paid to HM Revenue & Customs or reclaimed (**Difference between boxes 3 and 4**)	**Box 5**	
Total value of **sales** and all other outputs excluding any VAT. **Include your box 8 figure**	**Box 6**	
Total value of purchases and all other inputs excluding any VAT. **Include your box 9 figure**	**Box 7**	
Total value of all **supplies** of goods and related costs, excluding any VAT, to other **EC Member States**	**Box 8**	
Total value of all **acquisitions** of goods and related costs, excluding VAT, from other **EC Member States**	**Box 9**	

3 Communicating VAT information

3.1 Advising managers of the impact of VAT payments

Once the return has been completed it must be submitted to HMRC and any VAT owing paid over to HMRC. Most businesses submit and pay electronically.

In your assessment you may be asked to complete a short email to the financial accountant or another manager, giving the details of the return submission and the amount payable or receivable.

It will be important for the financial accountant (or other person responsible for managing the cash payments of the business) to know when the payment will be made, so that they can make sure that the funds are available in the bank account at the correct time.

You may be required to complete something along the following lines:

> ### Example
>
> To: Financial Accountant
> From: Dawn Jones
> Date: 17 April 20X1
> Subject: VAT return
>
> I have completed the VAT return for the quarter ended 31 March 20X1.
>
> The amount of VAT payable will be £23,561.42.
>
> This will be paid electronically by 7 May 20X1.
>
> If you need any further information please contact me.
>
> Best wishes
> Dawn (Junior Accountant)

3.2 Ethical implications

As mentioned in both chapters 1 and 6, it is important to adhere to the AAT's Professional Code of Ethics.

Advising managers of correct payment dates demonstrates professional competence and due care.

Members must act with integrity and resist any pressure to omit transactions or falsify dates.

Test your understanding 8

You are an accounting technician for a business.

You are preparing the VAT return for the quarter ended 30 June 20X8. In this quarter the business spent £2,400, including VAT, on a party for the 20 staff who all brought a guest.

Your supervisor has asked you to reclaim all the VAT on the cost of the party as in their words 'no one at HMRC will know if there were guests at the party or not'.

Which of the following is your correct response:

A   You do as your supervisor asks as it is their responsibility if VAT rules are broken.

B   You do as your supervisor asks but make a note in the file that you have done so.

C   You tell your supervisor that you cannot do as they ask as it is both a breach of VAT rules and your AAT Professional Code of Ethics.

 4 **Summary**

In this chapter the actual completion of the VAT return was considered. A business should keep a VAT account which summarises all of the VAT from the accounting records and this can be used to complete the first five boxes on the VAT return. The figure for VAT due to or from HM Revenue and Customs on the VAT return should equal the balance on the VAT account.

In order to complete the remaining boxes on the VAT return information will be required from the accounting records of the business, normally in the form of the day books.

As well as completing the VAT return you will need to be able to advise the relevant person of the payment or repayment needed.

Test your understanding answers

 ### Test your understanding 1

The correct answer is B.

The credit note due to a customer includes VAT of £13.50 (£81 × 20/120). If posted correctly this reduces output VAT. This has been included on the wrong side of the VAT account and hence is increasing the output VAT. It must be posted twice to the other side of the account to correct it. This has the effect of reducing the VAT due to HMRC by £27.

The purchase invoice includes VAT of £70 (£420 × 20/120). Including this in the VAT account will increase input VAT and hence reduce the VAT due to HMRC.

The net reduction is £97 (£27 + £70).

The corrected balance is therefore £3,375.56 (£3,472.56 – £97)

 ### Test your understanding 2

The correct answer is B.

The VAT return is showing £269.64 (£2,246.39 – £1,976.75) less VAT repayable than it should. Therefore, we are looking for an error that has overstated output tax or understated input tax.

Error A would mean that input VAT was overstated on the VAT return by £269.64 (£5,410.26 – £5,140.62), increasing the VAT repayable.

Error B – if treated correctly, a credit note to a customer reduces output tax. Lendl's error means that input tax has been decreased instead and in order to correct this, output tax must be decreased by twice the error i.e. £269.64 (£808.92 × 20/120 × 2).

Test your understanding 3

A	Sales	1
B	Cash sales	7
C	Credit notes issued	2
D	Purchases	6
E	Cash purchases	7 and 9
F	Credit notes received	4
G	Capital goods sold	8 or 1 (if an analysed sales day book)
H	Capital goods purchased	8 or 6 (if analysed)
I	Bad debt relief	3

Test your understanding 4

		£
VAT due in the period on sales and other outputs	Box 1	2,771.97
VAT due in the period on acquisitions from other EC Member States	Box 2	0.00
Total VAT due (the sum of boxes 1 and 2)	Box 3	2,771.97
VAT reclaimed in the period on purchases and other inputs, including acquisitions from the EC	Box 4	1,438.40
Net VAT to be paid to HM Revenue & Customs or reclaimed (Difference between boxes 3 and 4)	Box 5	1,333.57
Total value of sales and all other outputs excluding any VAT. Include your box 8 figure	Box 6	15,251
Total value of purchases and all other inputs excluding any VAT. Include your box 9 figure	Box 7	8,092
Total value of all supplies of goods and related costs, excluding any VAT, to other EC Member States	Box 8	0
Total value of all acquisitions of goods and related costs, excluding any VAT, from other EC Member States	Box 9	0

Workings

Box 1	£
VAT on sales	3,097.12
Less: VAT on credit notes	(325.15)
	2,771.97

Box 4	£
VAT on purchases	1,625.49
Less: VAT on credit notes	(187.09)
	1,438.40

Box 6	£
Standard-rated sales	15,485.60
Zero-rated sales	1,497.56
	16,983.16
Less: Credit notes	
Standard-rated	(1,625.77)
Zero-rated	(106.59)
Balance on sales & sales returns account	15,250.80

Box 7	£
Standard-rated purchases	8,127.45
Zero-rated purchases	980.57
	9,108.02
Less: Credit notes	
Standard-rated	(935.47)
Zero-rated	(80.40)
Balance on purchase & purchase returns account	8,092.15

Test your understanding 5

		£
VAT due in the period on **sales** and other outputs	Box 1	4,324.00
VAT due in the period on **acquisitions** from other **EU Member States**	Box 2	0.00
Total VAT due (**the sum of boxes 1 and 2**)	Box 3	4,324.00
VAT reclaimed in the period on **purchases** and other inputs, including acquisitions from the EU	Box 4	1,835.12
Net VAT to be paid to HM Revenue & Customs or reclaimed (**Difference between boxes 3 and 4**)	Box 5	2,488.88
Total value of **sales** and all other outputs excluding any VAT. **Include your box 8 figure**	Box 6	22,020
Total value of purchases and all other inputs excluding any VAT. **Include your box 9 figure**	Box 7	9,176
Total value of all **supplies** of goods and related costs, excluding any VAT, to other **EU Member States**	Box 8	0
Total value of all **acquisitions** of goods and related costs, excluding any VAT, from other **EU Member States**	Box 9	0

Workings for VAT return

		£
Box 1:	From VAT account	4,300.00
	Error on previous return	24.00
		4,324.00

Note that the output VAT total of £4,324.00 is not 20% of sales in the sales account of £22,020. This is because the sales figure is likely to be a mix of standard-rated plus zero-rated or exempt sales.

If you are given figures in ledger account form then you can assume they are correct amounts unless the question indicates otherwise.

Box 4:	From VAT account	£ 1,820.00
	Petty cash	15.12
		1,835.12

Box 7:	From Purchases account	£ 9,100
	Petty cash (£75.60 rounded up)	76
		9,176

Note that for Boxes 6 – 9, enter figures to the nearest £.

 Test your understanding 6

The correct answer is C.

Bad debt relief can be claimed after 6 months has elapsed from the date payment was due (or the date of supply if later).

In this case, 6 months after 15 March 20X6 is 15 September 20X6, which falls into the quarter ended 30 November 20X6.

✏️ Test your understanding 7

		£
VAT due in the period on **sales** and other outputs	**Box 1**	7,680.00
VAT due in the period on **acquisitions** from other **EC Member States**	**Box 2**	0.00
Total VAT due (**the sum of boxes 1 and 2**)	**Box 3**	7,680.00
VAT reclaimed in the period on **purchases** and other inputs, including acquisitions from the EC	**Box 4**	3,374.00
Net VAT to be paid to HM Revenue & Customs or reclaimed (**Difference between boxes 3 and 4**)	**Box 5**	4,306.00
Total value of **sales** and all other outputs excluding any VAT. **Include your box 8 figure**	**Box 6**	38,400
Total value of purchases and all other inputs excluding any VAT. **Include your box 9 figure**	**Box 7**	23,470
Total value of all **supplies** of goods and related costs, excluding any VAT, to other **EC Member States**	**Box 8**	0
Total value of all **acquisitions** of goods and related costs, excluding any VAT, from other **EC Member States**	**Box 9**	0

Workings for VAT return

		£
Box 4:	From PDB	3,294.00
	Bad debts (Note)	80.00
		3,374.00

		£
Box 7:	From PDB	16,470
	New car (£8,400 × 100/120)	7,000
		23,470

Note: Bad debts more than six months old = (£300.00 + £180.00) = £480.00
VAT = (20/120 × £480.00) = £80.00

Test your understanding 8

The correct answer is C.

It is important that you can demonstrate integrity and professional behaviour and are not swayed by pressure to act illegally and allow irrecoverable VAT to appear in the VAT return.

Overseas issues

Introduction

In the final chapter of this study text we are going to conclude our VAT studies by looking at how to deal with overseas transactions.

ASSESSMENT CRITERIA	CONTENTS
Identify and analyse relevant information on VAT (1.1)	1 Place of supply
Extract relevant data from the accounting records (2.1)	2 Goods – imports and exports
Calculate relevant input and output tax (2.2)	3 Goods – acquisitions and despatches
Calculate the VAT due to, or from, the relevant tax authority (2.3)	4 Supplies of services
Make adjustments and declarations for any errors or omissions identified in previous VAT periods (2.4)	
Complete and submit a VAT return and make any associated payment within statutory limits (2.5)	
Inform the appropriate person about VAT-related matters (4.1)	
Communicate information about VAT due to or from the tax authority (4.2)	

1 Place of supply

1.1 Introduction

VAT is a sales tax which is specifically levied within the European Union (EU). It therefore applies to sales within the EU but technically not to sales outside the EU (i.e. exports).

However, all purchases of goods or services made by EU businesses are in fact subject to VAT rules, whether purchased from within or outside the EU.

The rules for dealing with purchases from outside the EU can be complex, but you only require a broad understanding of how they are dealt with which is explained in this chapter.

Note that the European Union (EU) was previously known as the European Community (EC), and the VAT returns for completion in your assessment may still use the old term 'EC' or may use the new term. In our examples we use both terms to ensure familiarity with either term.

1.2 Place of supply

The place of supply rules help to decide how VAT is charged on overseas transactions. In broad terms the rules are as follows.

Supply of:

Goods These are treated as supplied in the country where the **goods originate**.

Services (a) Business to business (B2B)

(i.e. supplies to business customers)

The supply is treated as made in the country where the **customer is based**.

If the customer is based in the EU then VAT must be applied.

(b) Business to customer (B2C)

(i.e. supplies to non-business customers (e.g. to individuals) and businesses that are not registered for VAT)

The supply is treated as made in the country where the **supplier is based**.

If the supplier is based in the EU then VAT must be applied in the normal way.

There are exceptions to these rules for certain services such as accountancy and digital downloads but details of these rules are not required for your assessment.

Reference material

Information about the place of supply rules is included in the indirect tax reference material provided in the real assessment, so you do not need to learn it.

It can be found in the 'Place of supply' section.

You need to be familiar with the location and content of the material as in the assessment you will need to access the correct part of the reference material from a series of clickable links.

Why not look up the correct part of the indirect tax reference material in the appendix to this text book now?

---

2 Goods – imports and exports

2.1 Exports to non-EU members

Generally, goods exported from the United Kingdom to a non-EU country are technically not subject to VAT. However, they are treated as zero-rated supplies (i.e. it is a taxable supply, but no VAT is charged on them, even if there normally would be) provided there is documentary evidence of the export.

As no VAT needs to be charged, there will be no output tax to include in Box 1. This is the same for all zero-rated sales.

However these export sales are included with other sales in Box 6 of the return.

2.2 Imports from non-EU members

Goods that are imported from outside the EU have customs duty levied on them when they enter the country. Customs duty is outside the scope of this indirect tax paper and is not considered further.

However, even though no VAT is charged by the non-EU supplier on the goods, any goods that would be taxed at the standard rate of VAT if supplied in the United Kingdom are subject to VAT.

The amount payable is based on their value including customs duty.

This applies to all goods whether or not they are for business use. The aim of the charge is to treat foreign goods in the same way as home-produced goods.

The VAT is paid at the port of entry and the goods will typically not be released until it is paid.

If the imported goods are for business use and the business uses them to make taxable supplies, it can reclaim the VAT paid in the usual way as input tax on the VAT return (Box 4).

The cost of the goods purchased (excluding VAT) is included with other purchases in Box 7.

Note that provided the business is not partially exempt, there will be no overall net cost of VAT.

However, there will be a cash flow implication as the VAT normally has to be paid to HMRC before it can be recovered as input tax.

 Example

Meurig runs a UK VAT-registered business.

He imports a large amount of goods from outside the EU which would be standard-rated if bought in the UK.

All the goods he sells are standard-rated items.

In the quarter ended 31 December 20X1 he makes sales and purchases as follows:

	£
Sales to UK businesses	70,000
Export sales outside the EU	12,400
Purchases from UK businesses	38,500
Imports from outside the EU	17,450

All these figures exclude VAT.

What are the figures to include in Boxes 1, 4, 6 and 7?

Solution

		£
Box 1	VAT on standard-rated sales 20% × £70,000	14,000.00
Box 4	VAT on purchases 20% × (£38,500 + £17,450)	11,190.00
Box 6	All sales (£70,000 + £12,400)	82,400
Box 7	All purchases (£38,500 + £17,450)	55,950

The sales outside the EU are zero-rated so there is no VAT to include in Box 1. However, UK and export sales are included in Box 6.

Imports from outside the EU are treated like normal UK purchases from the point of view of the VAT return.

3 Goods – acquisitions and despatches

3.1 Exports and imports to and from countries within the EU

When both the selling and purchasing country are EU members, the rules differ according to whether or not the purchaser is a VAT-registered business.

Note that movements of goods between EU Member States are not known as imports and exports but as **acquisitions** and **despatches**.

In what follows we refer to HM Revenue and Customs ('HMRC') as the collecting authority, even though in different countries it will have a different name.

3.2 Sale to a VAT-registered business (B2B)

- When an EU member sells goods to a VAT-registered business in another EU country, it is the **buyer** who pays over the VAT to HMRC (or the equivalent in the buyer's country).

- Provided the seller has the buyer's VAT number, the seller sells the goods zero-rated to the buyer. The buyer will then pay VAT to HMRC at the appropriate rate. The buyer can also reclaim the VAT from HMRC.

We can summarise this as follows:

The seller

- The seller will supply the goods zero-rated.

- The seller makes no entries in Boxes 1 to 4 of the VAT return (in common with other zero-rated sales).

- The seller will enter the value of the sale with other sales in Box 6 **and** again in Box 8. Note the wording on the form helps you with this.

The buyer

- The VAT-registered buyer will pay the seller the sale price of the goods (excluding any VAT).

- The buyer will enter the VAT output tax in Box 2 of the return and the VAT input tax in Box 4 of the return. Thus, the net amount of VAT the buyer pays to HMRC is £Nil.

- The buyer will also enter the VAT-exclusive price of the goods in Box 7 (with the other purchases) and also in Box 9.

3.3 Sale to a buyer that is not VAT-registered (B2C)

- When a sale is made to a buyer that is not VAT-registered, the seller has to charge VAT at the standard rate.

- The buyer will pay the VAT-inclusive price to the seller.

- The entries on the return are the same as if selling to a UK customer. These sales are included in Box 6 but are **not** included in Box 8.

We can summarise this as follows:

The seller

- The seller supplies the goods and charges VAT. The seller enters the VAT in Box 1.

- The seller enters the VAT-exclusive price in Box 6.

The buyer

- The buyer pays the VAT-inclusive price to the seller and of course makes no entries in a VAT return because he is not VAT-registered.

- Note that if a UK business has a high level of such sales to another EU country, they may have to register for VAT in that other country.

  However, this is outside the scope of this assessment.

Example

Trystan runs a UK business selling Welsh handicraft items. He has recently started to sell goods overseas. All the goods he sells are standard-rated items.

In the quarter ended 31 December 20X1 he makes sales as follows:

	£
Sales to UK businesses	40,000
Sales to EU registered businesses	10,500
Sales to EU non-registered customers	21,000
Export sales outside the EU	12,400

All these figures exclude VAT.

What are the figures to include in Boxes 1, 6 and 8?

Solution

		£
Box 1	VAT on standard-rated sales 20% × (£40,000 + £21,000)	12,200.00
Box 6	All sales (£40,000 + £10,500 + £21,000 + £12,400)	83,900
Box 8	Sales to EU businesses	10,500

Test your understanding 1

The following accounts have been extracted from a company's ledgers

Date		Dr £	Cr £
Sales: UK			
30.6.X1	Sales day book		60,500
31.7.X1	Sales day book		89,510
31.8 X1	Sales day book		70,400
Sales: Export EU			
30.6.X1	Sales day book		15,150
31.7.X1	Sales day book		20,580
31.8 X1	Sales day book		17,890
Sales: Exports non-EU			
30.6.X1	Sales day book		8,500
31.7.X1	Sales day book		7,450
31.8 X1	Sales day book		10,100
Purchases: UK			
30.6.X1	Purchases day book	34,600	
31.7.X1	Purchases day book	31,590	
31.8 X1	Purchases day book	33,670	
VAT: Output tax			
30.6.X1	Sales day book		12,100.00
31.7.X1	Sales day book		17,902.00
31.8 X1	Sales day book		14,080.00
VAT: Input tax			
30.6.X1	Purchases day book	6,920.00	
31.7.X1	Purchases day book	6,318.00	
31.8 X1	Purchases day book	6,734.00	

Bad debt relief on a sales invoice for £6,000 including VAT is to be claimed this quarter.

The business overstated output VAT of £2,350 in the previous quarter and this must be corrected.

Exports within the EU were to VAT-registered customers.

Prepare the following VAT form 100 for the period.

		£
VAT due in the period on **sales** and other outputs	**Box 1**	
VAT due in the period on **acquisitions** from other **EU Member States**	**Box 2**	
Total VAT due (**the sum of boxes 1 and 2**)	**Box 3**	
VAT reclaimed in the period on **purchases** and other inputs, including acquisitions from the EU	**Box 4**	
Net VAT to be paid to HM Revenue & Customs or reclaimed (**Difference between boxes 3 and 4**)	**Box 5**	
Total value of **sales** and all other outputs excluding any VAT. **Include your box 8 figure**	**Box 6**	
Total value of purchases and all other inputs excluding any VAT. **Include your box 9 figure**	**Box 7**	
Total value of all **supplies** of goods and related costs, excluding any VAT, to other **EU Member States**	**Box 8**	
Total value of all **acquisitions** of goods and related costs, excluding any VAT, from other **EU Member States**	**Box 9**	

Test your understanding 2

Bettrys runs a UK business selling standard-rated pet accessories. She imports some items from overseas, both from other EU countries and from outside the EU.

In the quarter ended 31 December 20X1 her purchases are as follows:

	£
Purchases from UK businesses	27,400
Purchases from EU registered businesses	13,700
Purchases from outside the EU	18,800

All these figures exclude VAT.

What are the figures to include in Boxes 2, 4, 7 and 9?

 Test your understanding 3

Warhorse Ltd runs a UK business selling standard-rated horse-riding accessories.

The company imports some items from overseas, both from other EU countries and from outside the EU.

In the quarter ended 30 June 20X2 the details of purchases are as follows:

	£
Purchases from UK businesses	31,250
Purchases from EU registered businesses	7,650
Purchases from outside the EU	15,850

All these figures exclude VAT.

What are the figures to include in Boxes 2, 4, 7 and 9?

Test your understanding 4

You are given the following summaries of the sales and purchases daybooks, the cash book and the petty cash book of Defoe Ltd.

Use this information to complete the VAT return for the quarter ended 31 March 20X8.

DEFOE LIMITED : SALES DAY BOOK SUMMARY

JANUARY TO MARCH 20X8

	JAN £	FEB £	MAR £	TOTAL £
UK: ZERO-RATED	20,091.12	22,397.00	23,018.55	65,506.67
UK: STANDARD-RATED	15,682.30	12,914.03	15,632.98	44,229.31
OTHER EU	874.12	4,992.66	5,003.82	10,870.60
VAT	3,136.46	2,582.80	3,126.59	8,845.85
TOTAL	39,784.00	42,886.49	46,781.94	129,452.43

DEFOE LIMITED : PURCHASES DAY BOOK SUMMARY

JANUARY TO MARCH 20X8

	JAN £	FEB £	MAR £	TOTAL £
PURCHASES	14,532.11	20,914.33	15,461.77	50,908.21
DISTRIBUTION EXPENSES	4,229.04	3,761.20	5,221.43	13,211.67
ADMIN EXPENSES	5,123.08	2,871.45	3,681.62	11,676.15
OTHER EXPENSES	1,231.00	1,154.99	997.65	3,383.64
VAT	4,113.67	4,639.88	4,206.98	12,960.53
TOTAL	29,228.90	33,341.85	29,569.45	92,140.20

DEFOE LIMITED : CASH BOOK SUMMARY
JANUARY TO MARCH 20X8

	JAN £	FEB £	MAR £	TOTAL £
PAYMENTS:				
TO CREDITORS	12,901.37	15,312.70	18,712.44	46,926.51
TO PETTY CASH	601.40	555.08	623.81	1,780.29
WAGES/SALARIES	5,882.18	6,017.98	6,114.31	18,014.47
TOTAL	19,384.95	21,885.76	25,450.56	66,721.27
RECEIPTS:				
VAT FROM HMRC	2,998.01			2,998.01
FROM CUSTOMERS	29,312.44	34,216.08	36,108.77	99,637.29
TOTAL	32,310.45	34,216.08	36,108.77	102,635.30

DEFOE LIMITED : PETTY CASH BOOK SUMMARY
JANUARY TO MARCH 20X8

	JAN £	FEB £	MAR £	TOTAL £
PAYMENTS:				
STATIONERY	213.85	80.12	237.58	531.55
TRAVEL	87.34	76.50	102.70	266.54
OFFICE EXPENSES	213.66	324.08	199.51	737.25
VAT	86.55	74.38	84.02	244.95
TOTAL	601.40	555.08	623.81	1,780.29
RECEIPTS:				
FROM CASH BOOK	601.40	555.08	623.81	1,780.29

Blank VAT return for completion

		£
VAT due in the period on **sales** and other outputs	Box 1	
VAT due in the period on **acquisitions** from other **EC Member States**	Box 2	
Total VAT due (**the sum of boxes 1 and 2**)	Box 3	
VAT reclaimed in the period on **purchases** and other inputs, including acquisitions from the EC	Box 4	
Net VAT to be paid to HM Revenue & Customs or reclaimed (**Difference between boxes 3 and 4**)	Box 5	
Total value of **sales** and all other outputs excluding any VAT. **Include your box 8 figure**	Box 6	
Total value of purchases and all other inputs excluding any VAT. **Include your box 9 figure**	Box 7	
Total value of all **supplies** of goods and related costs, excluding any VAT, to other **EC Member States**	Box 8	
Total value of all **acquisitions** of goods and related costs, excluding any VAT, from other **EC Member States**	Box 9	

4 Supplies of services

4.1 Business to business transactions (B2B)

As explained in the place of supply rules, B2B supplies of services are treated as a supply made in the country where the **customer is based**.

Accordingly, if the customer is based:

In the EU: VAT at the appropriate rate in that country is charged but the 'reverse charge' procedure applies (4.2 below)

Outside the EU: The supplier will not have to account for any VAT as the supply is outside the scope of VAT.
The supplier will still include the sale in Box 6 of the return.

4.2 The reverse charge

Services supplied to businesses within the EU follow the 'reverse charge' principle.

The acquiring business is treated as if it had supplied the services to itself and VAT will be accounted for at the rate applicable to that type of supply in the customer's home country.

The vendor business includes the net value of the supply in Box 6.

Output tax must be paid by the acquiring business and included in Box 1 of the return. It can then be recovered by including it in Box 4 of the return.

The net value of the supply must then be included in Box 6 (sales) and Box 7 (purchases).

This is a 'paper' transaction with no cash flow implications. Provided the purchasing business is not partially exempt there will be no net cost to the business.

Example

Geraint runs a UK VAT-registered business. He buys services from overseas which would be standard-rated if bought in the UK. In the quarter ended 31 December 20X6 he buys services totalling £26,000 excluding VAT.

What are the figures to include in Boxes 1, 4, 6 and 7 in respect of these services?

Solution

		£
Box 1	VAT on standard-rated sales	
	20% × £26,000	5,200.00
Box 4	VAT on purchases	5,200.00
Box 6	Sales	26,000
Box 7	Purchases	26,000

 Reference material

Information about overseas aspects of VAT is included in the indirect tax reference material provided in the real assessment, so you do not need to learn it.

It can be found in the 'Place of supply', Transactions outside the UK' and 'Completing the VAT return' sections.

You need to be familiar with the location and content of the material as in the assessment you will need to access the correct part of the reference material from a series of clickable links.

Why not look up the correct part of the indirect tax reference material in the appendix to this text book now?

4.3 Business to customer transactions (B2C)

Supplies of services to a non-business customer (e.g. an individual) or an unregistered business are treated as a supply made in the country where the **supplier is based**.

Accordingly, as the focus in this assessment will be on a UK supplier, VAT is applied in the normal way as if the supply is made within the UK.

5 Test your understanding

 Test your understanding 5

The following accounts have been extracted from the business's ledgers for the quarter ended 31 August 20X0.

Sales account

Date 20X0	Ref	Debit £	Date 20X0	Ref	Credit £
31/08	Balance c/d	700,600.00	01/06 – 31/08	Sales day book – UK sales	672,600.00
			01/06 – 31/08	Sales day book – EU despatches	28,000.00
	Total	700,600.00		Total	700,600.00

Purchases account

Date 20X0	Ref	Debit £	Date 20X0	Ref	Credit £
01/06 – 31/08	Purchases day book – UK purchases	230,800.00	31/08	Balance c/d	271,800.00
01/06 – 31/08	Purchases day book – imports	41,000.00			
	Total	271,800.00		Total	271,800.00

VAT account

Date 20X0	Ref	Debit £	Date 20X0	Ref	Credit £
01/06 – 31/08	Purchases day book	40,390.00	01/06 – 31/08	Sales day book	100,205.00

You are also told that bad debt relief is to be claimed in this quarter for £4,200.00 VAT, and despatches are to a VAT-registered business in Germany.

Prepare the following VAT form 100 for the period.

		£
VAT due in the period on **sales** and other outputs	**Box 1**	
VAT due in the period on **acquisitions** from other **EU Member States**	**Box 2**	
Total VAT due (**the sum of boxes 1 and 2**)	**Box 3**	
VAT reclaimed in the period on **purchases** and other inputs, including acquisitions from the EU	**Box 4**	
Net VAT to be paid to HM Revenue & Customs or reclaimed (**Difference between boxes 3 and 4**)	**Box 5**	
Total value of **sales** and all other outputs excluding any VAT. **Include your box 8 figure**	**Box 6**	
Total value of purchases and all other inputs excluding any VAT. **Include your box 9 figure**	**Box 7**	
Total value of all **supplies** of goods and related costs, excluding any VAT, to other **EU Member States**	**Box 8**	
Total value of all **acquisitions** of goods and related costs, excluding any VAT, from other **EU Member States**	**Box 9**	

Test your understanding 6

You are required to complete a VAT return for Coleman Limited in respect of the quarter ended 31 December 20X8.

You are given the following information to assist you in this task:

1   Of the external sales of £916,000 made during the quarter ended 31 December 20X8, a total of £65,000 relates to despatches of goods to EU countries, to VAT-registered customers.

    The remainder of this quarter's sales was of standard-rated sales to UK customers. All sales figures given exclude VAT.

2   Total purchases by the company in the quarter amounted to £310,000 of standard-rated inputs, and £23,000 of zero-rated inputs (both figures stated are exclusive of VAT).

    All of these purchases were from within the UK.

3   The sales figures for October 20X8 include an invoice for standard-rated goods with a value, excluding VAT, of £3,200.

    These goods were actually despatched in September 20X8 and should have been accounted for in the VAT return for the previous quarter, but were omitted in error.

4   A debt of £624, inclusive of VAT, was written off as bad during the month of December 20X8.

    The related sale was made in February 20X8. Bad debt relief is now to be claimed.

Prepare the following VAT form 100 for the period.

		£
VAT due in the period on **sales** and other outputs	**Box 1**	
VAT due in the period on **acquisitions** from other **EC Member States**	**Box 2**	
Total VAT due (**the sum of boxes 1 and 2**)	**Box 3**	
VAT reclaimed in the period on **purchases** and other inputs, including acquisitions from the EC	**Box 4**	
Net VAT to be paid to HM Revenue & Customs or reclaimed (**Difference between boxes 3 and 4**)	**Box 5**	
Total value of **sales** and all other outputs excluding any VAT. **Include your box 8 figure**	**Box 6**	
Total value of purchases and all other inputs excluding any VAT. **Include your box 9 figure**	**Box 7**	
Total value of all **supplies** of goods and related costs, excluding any VAT, to other **EC Member States**	**Box 8**	
Total value of all **acquisitions** of goods and related costs, excluding any VAT, from other **EC Member States**	**Box 9**	

Test your understanding 7

You are an accounting technician for a business reporting to the financial accountant.

You have completed the following VAT return for the quarter ended 31 March 20X0.

VAT return for the quarter ended 31 March 20X0		£
VAT due in the period on **sales** and other outputs	Box 1	142,371.25
VAT due in the period on **acquisitions** from other **EU Member States**	Box 2	11,340.00
Total VAT due (**the sum of boxes 1 and 2**)	Box 3	153,711.25
VAT reclaimed in the period on **purchases** and other inputs, including acquisitions from the EU	Box 4	57,785.00
Net VAT to be paid to HM Revenue & Customs or reclaimed (**Difference between boxes 3 and 4**)	Box 5	95,926.25
Total value of **sales** and all other outputs excluding any VAT. **Include your box 8 figure**	Box 6	859,450
Total value of purchases and all other inputs excluding any VAT. **Include your box 9 figure**	Box 7	395,000
Total value of all **supplies** of goods and related costs, excluding any VAT, to other **EU Member States**	Box 8	45,900
Total value of all **acquisitions** of goods and related costs, excluding any VAT, from other **EU Member States**	Box 9	64,800

The business does not operate any special accounting schemes.

Today's date is 20 April 20X0.

Complete this email to the financial accountant advising her of the amount of VAT that will be paid or received and the due date.

Where options are given select one.

To: **Financial accountant/accounting technician/HMRC**

From: **Financial accountant/accounting technician/HMRC**

Date: **31 March 20X0/20 April 20X0/ 30 April 20X0/7 May 20X0**

Subject : Completed VAT return

Please be advised that I have just completed the VAT return for the quarter ended:

31 March 20X0/20 April 20X0/ 30 April 20X0/ 7 May 20X0.

The amount of VAT **receivable/payable** will be £.........................

Please arrange to pay this electronically to arrive no later than 30 April 20X0/

Please arrange to pay this electronically to arrive no later than 7 May 20X0/

Please arrange to pay this electronically to arrive no later than 31 May 20X0/

Please expect to see this as a receipt in our bank account in due course.

6 Summary

In this final chapter the rules on dealing with sales and purchases overseas have been covered.

They can be summarised as follows for a UK business that only makes standard-rated sales and purchases.

Goods

Type of transaction	Treatment on VAT return	
Sales outside EU (exports)	Zero-rated	Include sales in Box 6
Sales within EU – to VAT-registered customers (despatches)	Zero-rated	Include sales in Box 6 and in Box 8
Sales within EU – to customers that are not VAT-registered (despatches)	Standard-rated	Include VAT in Box 1 Include sales in Box 6
Purchases from outside EU (imports)	Standard-rated	Include VAT in Box 4 Include purchases in Box 7
Purchases from within EU (acquisitions)	Standard-rated	Include VAT in both Box 2 and Box 4 Include purchases in both Box 7 and Box 9

Services

Type of transaction	Treatment on VAT return	
B2B sales	Outside scope of VAT	Include sales in Box 6
B2C sales	Standard-rated	Include as a sale and put output VAT in Box 1 and the net sale value in Box 6
B2B purchases	Reverse charge	Include as a purchase and put input VAT in Box 4 and the net purchase value in Box 7

Test your understanding answers

Test your understanding 1

		£
VAT due in the period on **sales** and other outputs	Box 1	41,732.00
VAT due in the period on **acquisitions** from other **EU Member States**	Box 2	0.00
Total VAT due (**the sum of boxes 1 and 2**)	Box 3	41,732.00
VAT reclaimed in the period on **purchases** and other inputs, including acquisitions from the EU	Box 4	20,972.00
Net VAT to be paid to HM Revenue & Customs or reclaimed (**Difference between boxes 3 and 4**)	Box 5	20,760.00
Total value of **sales** and all other outputs excluding any VAT. **Include your box 8 figure**	Box 6	300,080
Total value of purchases and all other inputs excluding any VAT. **Include your box 9 figure**	Box 7	99,860
Total value of all **supplies** of goods and related costs, excluding any VAT, to other **EU Member States**	Box 8	53,620
Total value of all **acquisitions** of goods and related costs, excluding any VAT, from other **EU Member States**	Box 9	0

Workings for VAT return

		£
Box 1:	From VAT account – output tax (£12,100.00 + £17,902.00 + £14,080.00)	44,082.00
	Output VAT overstated	(2,350.00)
		41,732.00

As the error is a single error affecting output tax it is adjusted by subtracting the overstatement from Box 1.

		£
Box 4:	From VAT account – input tax (£6,920.00 + £6,318.00 + £6,734.00)	19,972.00
	Bad debt relief (£6,000 × 20/120)	1,000.00
		20,972.00
Box 6:	Sales: UK (£60,500 + £89,510 + £70,400)	220,410
	Sales: Export EU (£15,150 + £20,580 + £17,890)	53,620
	Sales: Export non-EU (£8,500 + £7,450 + £10,100)	26,050
		300,080
Box 7:	Purchases (£34,600 + £31,590 + £33,670)	99,860

Test your understanding 2

Box 2	VAT on acquisitions from other EU countries	
	(20% × £13,700)	£2,740.00
Box 4	VAT reclaimed	
	20% × (£27,400 + £13,700 + £18,800)	£11,980.00
Box 7	Total purchases	
	(£27,400 + £13,700 + £18,800)	£59,900
Box 9	Purchases from other EU countries	£13,700

Test your understanding 3

		£
Box 2	VAT on acquisitions from other EU countries	
	(20% × £7,650)	1,530.00
Box 4	VAT reclaimed	
	20% × (£31,250 + £7,650 + £15,850)	10,950.00
Box 7	Total purchases	
	(£31,250 + £7,650 + £15,850)	54,750
Box 9	Purchases from other EU countries	7,650

Test your understanding 4

Defoe Ltd – VAT return for the quarter ended 31 March 20X8

		£
VAT due in the period on **sales** and other outputs	**Box 1**	8,845.85
VAT due in the period on **acquisitions** from other **EC Member States**	**Box 2**	0.00
Total VAT due (**the sum of boxes 1 and 2**)	**Box 3**	8,845.85
VAT reclaimed in the period on **purchases** and other inputs, including acquisitions from the EC	**Box 4**	13,205.48
Net VAT to be paid to HM Revenue & Customs or reclaimed (**Difference between boxes 3 and 4**)	**Box 5**	4,359.63
Total value of **sales** and all other outputs excluding any VAT. **Include your box 8 figure**	**Box 6**	120,607
Total value of purchases and all other inputs excluding any VAT. **Include your box 9 figure**	**Box 7**	80,715
Total value of all **supplies** of goods and related costs, excluding any VAT, to other **EC Member States**	**Box 8**	10,871
Total value of all **acquisitions** of goods and related costs, excluding any VAT, from other **EC Member States**	**Box 9**	0

Workings for VAT return

		£
Box 4:	From Purchase day book	12,960.53
	From Petty cash book	244.95
		13,205.48

		£
Box 6:	Total from sales day book	129,452.43
	Less: VAT included	(8,845.85)
		120,606.58

		£
Box 7:	Purchase day book total	92,140.20
	Less: VAT included	(12,960.53)
	Petty cash book total	1,780.29
	Less: VAT included	(244.95)
		80,715.01

Test your understanding 5

		£
VAT due in the period on **sales** and other outputs	Box 1	100,205.00
VAT due in the period on **acquisitions** from other **EU Member States**	Box 2	0.00
Total VAT due (**the sum of boxes 1 and 2**)	Box 3	100,205.00
VAT reclaimed in the period on **purchases** and other inputs, including acquisitions from the EU	Box 4	44,590.00
Net VAT to be paid to HM Revenue & Customs or reclaimed (**Difference between boxes 3 and 4**)	Box 5	55,615.00
Total value of **sales** and all other outputs excluding any VAT. **Include your box 8 figure**	Box 6	700,600
Total value of purchases and all other inputs excluding any VAT. **Include your box 9 figure**	Box 7	271,800
Total value of all **supplies** of goods and related costs, excluding any VAT, to other **EU Member States**	Box 8	28,000
Total value of all **acquisitions** of goods and related costs, excluding any VAT, from other **EU Member States**	Box 9	0

Workings

Box 4	£
VAT on purchases from VAT account	40,390.00
VAT bad debt relief	4,200.00
	44,590.00

Test your understanding 6

		£
VAT due in the period on **sales** and other outputs	**Box 1**	170,200.00
VAT due in the period on **acquisitions** from other **EC Member States**	**Box 2**	0.00
Total VAT due (**the sum of boxes 1 and 2**)	**Box 3**	170,200.00
VAT reclaimed in the period on **purchases** and other inputs, including acquisitions from the EC	**Box 4**	62,104.00
Net VAT to be paid to HM Revenue & Customs or reclaimed (**Difference between boxes 3 and 4**)	**Box 5**	108,096.00
Total value of **sales** and all other outputs excluding any VAT. **Include your box 8 figure**	**Box 6**	916,000
Total value of purchases and all other inputs excluding any VAT. **Include your box 9 figure**	**Box 7**	333,000
Total value of all **supplies** of goods and related costs, excluding any VAT, to other **EC Member States**	**Box 8**	65,000
Total value of all **acquisitions** of goods and related costs, excluding any VAT, from other **EC Member States**	**Box 9**	0

Workings for VAT return

		£
Box 1:	External sales	916,000
	Less: Exports to EU countries (zero-rated)	(65,000)
	Standard-rated sales	851,000
	Output VAT (£851,000 × 20%)	170,200.00

		£
Box 4:	VAT on standard-rated purchases (£310,000 × 20%)	62,000.00
	Bad debt relief (£624 × 20/120)	104.00
		62,104.00

		£
Box 7:	Standard-rated inputs	310,000
	Zero-rated inputs	23,000
		333,000

Note that no adjustment is needed to the figures given in the question to calculate the numbers to be entered in the VAT return.

This is because the error does not need to be corrected by separate disclosure. The value of the error is below £10,000 so it can be corrected on this period's return.

The error is that output tax in the previous quarter was understated because a sales invoice was left out. However, the invoice has already been included in the total of outputs given in the question and hence output tax for this quarter, so does not need to be included again.

Test your understanding 7

To:	**Financial accountant**
From:	**Accounting technician**
Date:	**20 April 20X0**
Subject :	Completed VAT return

Please be advised that I have just completed the VAT return for the quarter ended:

31 March 20X0

The amount of VAT **payable** will be £............95,926.25..............

Please arrange to pay this electronically to arrive no later than 7 May 20X0

MOCK ASSESSMENT

1 Mock assessment questions

This assessment has 8 tasks.

You should therefore attempt and aim to complete EVERY task.

Each task is independent. You will not need to refer to your answers to previous tasks.

Read every task carefully to make sure you understand what is required.

Where the date is relevant, it is given in the task data.

Never **use minus signs or brackets to indicate negative numbers UNLESS task instructions say otherwise.**

You must use a full stop to indicate a decimal point.

Task 1 (6 marks)

(a) **Which two of the following statements about unregistered businesses are true?**   **(3 marks)**

(i) A business does not need to check its turnover for registration purposes until it has been trading for at least 12 months.

(ii) A business which makes a mixture of taxable and exempt supplies has to register when its taxable turnover for the last 12 months exceeds £85,000.

(iii) A business which has an annual turnover of £86,000 of standard-rated and exempt supplies can apply to be exempted from registration.

(iv) Owen runs two separate sole trader businesses each with standard-rated taxable turnover of £45,000 over the last 12 months. He must register for VAT.

A (i) and (ii)

B (ii) and (iii)

C (i) and (iv)

D (ii) and (iv)

(b) A trader who makes wholly zero-rated supplies can apply to be exempt from registration.

Choose ONE reason why the business might prefer not to be registered.   **(1 mark)**

A   It makes their prices cheaper for non-registered customers

B   If it has a very low level of input VAT

C   They do not have to charge VAT to customers

(c) Xander's business, which commenced on 1 February 20X7, is currently not registered for VAT.

Monthly turnover consists of

–   standard-rated supplies of £5,500

–   zero-rated supplies of £4,100

–   exempt supplies of £2,900

Assuming Xander does not register until required to do so, from when will his registration for VAT be effective?   **(2 marks)**

A   1 September 20X7

B   1 October 20X7

C   1 November 20X7

D   1 December 20X7

Task 2 (9 marks)

(a) Badella Ltd has returned some faulty goods to Lane plc and issued Lane plc with a debit note.

What is the effect on VAT of processing this debit note in the books of Badella Ltd?   **(2 marks)**

Select ONE answer.

A   Input tax will increase

B   Input tax will decrease

C   Output tax will increase

D   Output tax will decrease

(b)   A registered business supplies goods that are a mixture of standard-rated and exempt.

Which of the following statements is true?   **(2 marks)**

Select ONE answer.

A   All the input VAT relating to standard-rated goods can be reclaimed but never any relating to exempt supplies

B   None of the input VAT can be reclaimed

C   All of the input VAT can be reclaimed

D   All of the input VAT can be reclaimed providing certain (de minimis) conditions are met

(c)   **Which of the following are required to be shown on a VAT tax invoice for a UK supply?**   **(3 marks)**

Tick one box for each line

	Required	Not required
Supplier's name and address		
Customer's name and address		
Customer's registration number		
Method of delivery		
Separate total of any zero-rated goods included in the sale		
Any discount offered		
Delivery note number		
Total amount of VAT charged		
General terms of trade		

(d)   Jake sells goods to Ball Ltd on a sale or return basis. The goods are delivered to Ball Ltd on 4 March. The company has until 30 June in that year to decide whether to keep or return the goods.

Ball Ltd notifies Jake on 10 June that they will keep the goods.

Jake invoices Ball Ltd with an invoice dated 20 June.

What is the tax point date?   **(2 marks)**

A   4 March

B   10 June

C   20 June

D   30 June

Task 3 (5 marks)

Jacky runs a small business as a newsagent and has adopted the flat rate scheme for VAT.

In the year to 30 September 20X1 her figures for sales and purchases are as follows:

Standard-rated sales (including VAT)	£69,000
Zero-rated sales	£10,000
Standard-rated purchases (including VAT)	£18,500

The flat rate percentage for her trade is 9%. Jacky's business is not a limited cost business.

(a)   **What is her VAT payable under the flat rate scheme?**   **(2 marks)**

A   £5,445.00

B   £4,545.00

C   £7,110.00

D   £6,210.00

(b)   **Can Jacky also join the cash accounting scheme?**   **(1 mark)**

A   Yes

B   No

(c)   **Which of the following statements about the flat rate scheme are true?**

Tick one box in each line.   **(2 marks)**

	True	False
A discount of 1% is given from the flat rate percentage in the first year of registration		
You do not have to record how much VAT you charge on every sale in your accounts		
You can join the scheme provided your total turnover (including exempt supplies) is below £150,000		
Using the flat rate scheme is beneficial if you make a high level of zero-rated sales		
Budgeting for cash flow is easier as you know what percentage of your turnover is payable to HMRC		

Task 4 (9 marks)

(a)   **On which of the following purchases of vehicles, bought by registered businesses, can input VAT be reclaimed?**   **(3 marks)**

Tick one box on each line.

	Reclaim	No reclaim
A car bought for use by Bert, a sole trader. He plans to use the car 60% for his business and 40% privately.		
A car bought by Alana for use solely in her taxi business.		
A car bought by Sheard Ltd for general use as a pool car by all its employees.		
A car bought by Bee Ltd for the sole use of its managing director who uses the car for all his business and private use.		
A van bought by Dennis for use by one of his site foremen.		

(b)   X plc has discovered that VAT of £24,000 on a sales invoice of £120,000 (VAT-exclusive) was omitted from the last VAT return.

No correction has yet been made for this error.

The current quarter's VAT return has a Box 6 figure of £2,750,000.

Which of the following statements is true?   **(1 mark)**

A   The error is small enough to include on the current VAT return.

B   The error must be separately notified to HMRC.

(c)   **Which of the following statements about reclaiming VAT on motor expenses for a registered business is true?**

Select one answer.   **(2 marks)**

A   A business can reclaim all input VAT on fuel for business and private use

B   VAT on fuel for private motoring can only be reclaimed if the business keeps proper records of business and private mileage and pays the appropriate VAT fuel scale charge

C   VAT on fuel for private motoring can be reclaimed if the business pays the appropriate VAT fuel scale charge

D   A business cannot reclaim any VAT on fuel if part of it is used for private motoring

(d)   Zee Ltd is a VAT-registered business. Their VAT return for the quarter ended 31 March 20X1 is submitted online on 5 May 20X1. They pay their VAT by bank transfer on 10 May.

Which one of the following statements is true?   **(2 marks)**

A   As the VAT has been paid late a surcharge liability notice will be issued by HMRC covering the period up to 10 May 20X2

B   The VAT return was due on 30 April 20X1 and has been submitted late

C   If Zee Ltd had chosen to pay VAT owing by direct debit then their payment on 10 May would not have been late

(e)   Chapman is a VAT-registered business making a mix of standard and zero-rated supplies.

On 1 June 20X8 they start making exempt supplies and reduce the amount of standard-rated supplies they make.

Which one of the following statements is true?   **(1 mark)**

A   This change will be reflected when Chapman prepares the next VAT return so they do not have to notify HMRC.

B   This change should be notified to HMRC within 30 days.

Task 5 (7 marks)

(a) A VAT-registered business makes a standard-rated supply of crafting goods of £925. This figure is exclusive of VAT. A trade discount of 5% is given.

What is the correct amount of VAT to be shown on the invoice?

(2 marks)

A   £185.00

B   £154.16

C   £175.75

D   £146.45

(b) A VAT-registered business completed its VAT return which shows VAT owed to HMRC of £3,780.50.

The VAT account at the end of the same period correctly shows a balance of VAT due of £3,450.90.

Which of the following explains the difference?   (2 marks)

Choose ONE option.

A   Input VAT of £329.60 which was over claimed in the previous period has not been deducted in the VAT return

B   VAT of £329.60 on sales returns has not been included in the VAT return

(c) A business which consistently pays over £3,000 of VAT to HMRC each quarter has received a debit note from a customer for £393 (VAT-inclusive).

What will be the effect of processing this debit note on the VAT liability for this quarter?   (2 marks)

A   VAT due to HMRC will increase by £65.50

B   VAT due to HMRC will decrease by £65.50

C   VAT due to HMRC will increase by £78.60

D   VAT due to HMRC will decrease by £78.60

(d) A business runs a promotion where it offers to pay the customer's VAT.

Meera buys goods paying £90 to the business.

Calculate much VAT should be accounted for?   (1 mark)

Task 6 (7 marks)

(a) A business which makes only standard-rated supplies wrote off the following bad debts on 31.1.20X3.

Date payment due	Amount (VAT-inclusive) £
20.2.20X2	543.60
15.4.20X2	950.40
17.11.20X2	1,100.00

Calculate the amount of bad debt relief that can be claimed in the quarter to 31 March 20X3. **(3 marks)**

(b) **How should bad debt relief be claimed in the VAT return**

(1 mark)

A   Include in Box 1

B   Include in Box 4

(c) The VAT account of a business is currently showing:

Output tax of   £79,562.68

Input tax of   £47,083.21

No adjustments have yet been made for the following:

Fuel scale charges with total VAT of £890

Purchase of a van for the business costing £10,690 before VAT

What figures should appear in the VAT return? **(3 marks)**

(i)   Box 1 ....

(ii)   Box 4 ....

Task 7 (17 marks)

The following information has been extracted from the books and records of Timms Ltd, a small company that manufactures electrical components for the quarter ended 31 December 20X0.

UK SALES					
Date	Reference	Debit £	Date	Reference	Credit £
			31.12.	Standard-rated sales	186,468
31.12.	Balance c/d	213,410	31.12.	Zero-rated sales	26,942
	Total	213,410			213,410

EU SALES					
Date	Reference	Debit £	Date	Reference	Credit £
			31.12	VAT-registered customers	43,789
31.12	Balance c/d	54,789	31.12	Non-registered customers	11,000
	Total	54,789		Total	54,789

PURCHASES (UK)					
Date	Reference	Debit £	Date	Reference	Credit £
31.12	Standard-rated	96,421			
			31.12	Balance c/d	96,421
	Total	96,421		Total	96,421

VAT ACCOUNT (incomplete)					
Date	Reference	Debit £	Date	Reference	Credit £
31.12	Purchases (UK)	19,284.20	31.12	Sales (UK)	37,293.60
			31.12	Sales (EU)	2,200.00

- As well as the UK purchases, Timms Ltd has made acquisitions from EU VAT-registered suppliers of £15,390. This figure excludes VAT and is all for supplies that would be standard-rated in the UK.

- Bad debt relief of £853.33 VAT is to be claimed.

- In the previous quarter the VAT on a sales invoice of £10,500, excluding VAT, for a standard-rated sale to a UK customer was left out by mistake.

- VAT is payable by electronic bank transfer.

Complete Boxes 1 to 9 of the VAT return for the quarter ended 31 December 20X0.   (17 marks)

		£
VAT due in this period on **sales** and other outputs	Box 1	
VAT due in this period on **acquisitions** from other **EU Member States**	Box 2	
Total VAT due (**the sum of boxes 1 and 2**)	Box 3	
VAT reclaimed in the period on **purchases** and other inputs, including acquisitions from the EU	Box 4	
Net VAT to be paid to HM Revenue & Customs or reclaimed by you (**Difference between boxes 3 and 4**)	Box 5	
Total value of **sales** and all other outputs excluding any VAT. **Include your box 8 figure**	Box 6	
Total value of purchases and all other inputs excluding any VAT. **Include your box 9 figure**	Box 7	
Total value of all **supplies** of goods and related costs, excluding any VAT, to other **EU Member States**	Box 8	
Total value of all **acquisitions** of goods and related costs, excluding any VAT, from other **EU Member States**	Box 9	

Task 8 (10 marks)

(a) You are a junior accountant.

Complete the following email to the financial accountant of Power Ltd advising of the amount of VAT that will be paid or received and the due date for the online filing of the quarterly return to 31.12.20X0. **(7 marks)**

The figure in Box 3 of the return is £28,478.96

The figure in Box 4 of the return is £44,999.40

The business does not pay by direct debit.

Email

To:

From:

Date: 15.1.X1

Subject:

Please be advised that I have just completed the VAT return for the quarter ended (...........................).

The return must be filed by (.........................).

The amount of VAT **(payable/receivable)** will be (£...............................).

This will be **(paid electronically by ..../received directly into our bank account).**

Kind regards

(b) The accountant has replied to you with the following comment.

"The business is a bit short of cash this month so can you look at the return and see if there is anything we can do to shift some of the output tax into the next quarter".

Which of the following is not a suitable response?   **(3 marks)**

A   The accountant is my boss so I must do as he asks.

B   Making any adjustments without justification would be unethical.

C   I could recheck my figures to see if any items correctly belong to another period.

KAPLAN PUBLISHING

2 Mock assessment answers

Task 1

(a) The correct answer is D.

    (i) Is incorrect as a new business must check its turnover at the end of every month as it may reach the registration threshold before the end of their first 12 months of trading.

    (iii) is incorrect as it is only a business making wholly zero-rated supplies that can apply to be exempt from registration.

(b) The correct answer is B.

As the business makes wholly zero-rated supplies it would be charging VAT at 0% if it were registered and can recover any input VAT suffered.

This has no effect on its prices and the amount it charges its customers and therefore A and C are incorrect.

However, if it has a low level of input VAT to recover, it may not want to be registered as the administrative burden and costs may outweigh the benefit of input VAT recovery.

(c) The correct answer is D.

The total taxable supplies (standard and zero-rated) exceeds the registration threshold at the end of October.

HMRC must be notified by 30 November and registration takes effect on 1 December.

Exempt supplies are not taxable supplies and are ignored when determining the registration date.

Task 2

(a) The correct answer is B.

A debit note in the books of the issuing business has the same effect as a purchase credit note. It will reduce input VAT.

(b) The correct answer is D.

(c)   VAT invoice

	Required	Not required
Supplier's name and address	✓	
Customer's name and address	✓	
Customer's registration number		✓
Method of delivery		✓
Separate total of any zero-rated goods included in the sale	✓	
Any discount offered	✓	
Delivery note number		✓
Total amount of VAT charged	✓	
General terms of trade		✓

(d)   The correct answer is C.

The basic tax point for goods sent out on sale or return is the earlier of:

–   the date the goods are accepted (i.e. 10 June), or

–   the cut-off date for accepting the goods (provided this is no longer than 1 year after delivery) (i.e. 30 June)

This would make the basic tax point the 10 June.

However, as an invoice has been raised within 14 days of the basic tax point, the actual tax point date is moved to the date of the invoice under the 14 day rule.

Task 3

(a)   The correct answer is C.

(£69,000 + £10,000) × 9% = £7,110.00

Under the flat rate scheme the VAT payable to HMRC is calculated as a flat rate percentage of the total turnover including VAT.

(b)   The correct answer is B.

A trader cannot join both the flat rate scheme and the cash accounting scheme. However, when joining the flat rate scheme it is possible to request that calculations are made on a cash basis.

(c)   Flat rate scheme

	True	False
A discount of 1% is given from the flat rate percentage in the first year of registration	✓	
You do not have to record how much VAT you charge on every sale in your accounts	✓	
You can join the scheme provided your total turnover (including exempt supplies) is below £150,000		✓
Using the flat rate scheme is beneficial if you make a high level of zero-rated sales		✓
Budgeting for cash flow is easier as you know what percentage of your turnover is payable to HMRC	✓	

You can join the flat rate scheme provided your **taxable** turnover is below £150,000.

The flat rate percentage is calculated based on a typical business in that trade sector. If a business makes higher zero-rated sales than typical for that sector, they will pay more VAT under the flat rate scheme.

Task 4

(a)   Input tax reclaim on vehicles

	Reclaim	No reclaim
A car bought for use by Bert, a sole trader. He plans to use the car 60% for his business and 40% privately.		✓
A car bought by Alana for use solely in her taxi business.	✓	
A car bought by Sheard Ltd for general use as a pool car by all its employees.	✓	
A car bought by Bee Ltd for the sole use of its managing director who uses the car for all his business and private use.		✓
A van bought by Dennis for use by one of his site foremen.	✓	

(b) The correct answer is A.

Errors between £10,000 and £50,000 can be included on the VAT return provided they are no more than 1% of the Box 6 figure.

In this case, 1% of £2,750,000 is £27,500.

(c) The correct answer is C.

A business can reclaim VAT on all its fuel, both business and private, provided they pay the appropriate fuel scale charge for each vehicle.

It is not a requirement to keep proper records of the split between business and private mileage (unless only business mileage is being claimed).

(d) The correct answer is C.

Payments by direct debit are due 3 working days after the normal 7 day deadline so payment by 10 May could not be late.

A is false. The payment has been made late and a surcharge liability notice would be issued but it would cover the 12 months up to 31 March 20X2.

B is false because the online return would not be due until 7 May.

(e) The correct answer is B.

Changes which affect registration details including a change in types of supply must be notified to HMRC within 30 days.

Task 5

(a) The correct answer is C.

When a discount is offered, VAT must be calculated on the discounted price.

	£
Value of the supply	925.00
Less: 5% trade discount	(46.25)
Net value for VAT	878.75
VAT at 20%	175.75

Alternative calculation:
(£925.00 × 95%) at 20%   175.75

INDIRECT TAX

(b)   B is the correct answer.

The VAT return is showing VAT due of £329.60 more than the correct figure.

If a previous over claim of input VAT of £329.60 had not been included in this return, then Box 4 would need to be reduced and the VAT due per the VAT return would be increased.

VAT on sales returns should be deducted from the output VAT in Box 1 and would reduce the VAT due to HMRC. If the VAT on sales returns was omitted from the return, the figure for VAT due to HMRC would be higher than the correct figure.

(c)   The correct answer is B

A debit note from a customer would be processed in the same way as a sales credit note (i.e. deducted from output tax) and hence reduce VAT due.

As the amount is VAT-inclusive it must be multiplied by 20/120 to find the VAT of £65.50 (£393 × 20/120).

(d)   The £90 will be treated as VAT-inclusive. Therefore £15.00 (£90 × 20/120) output VAT should be accounted for.

Task 6

(a)   Bad debt relief = £249.00

(£543.60 + £950.40) × 20/120 (or use 1/6) = £249.00

Amounts receivable from customers are recorded gross (i.e. at the amount due from the customer including VAT).

VAT is found in a VAT-inclusive figure by multiplying by 20/120 or 1/6.

The debt of £1,100 due on 17.11.X2 is too recent to claim bad debt relief.

(b)   The correct answer is B.

(c)   (i)   Box 1   (£79,562.68 + £890) = £80,452.68

(ii)   Box 4   (£47,083.21 + (£10,690 × 20%)) = £49,221.21

Task 7

VAT return

		£
VAT due in the period on **sales** and other outputs	Box 1	41,593.60
VAT due in the period on **acquisitions** from other **EU Member States**	Box 2	3,078.00
Total VAT due (**the sum of boxes 1 and 2**)	Box 3	44,671.60
VAT reclaimed in the period on **purchases** and other inputs, including acquisitions from the EU	Box 4	23,215.53
Net VAT to be paid to HM Revenue & Customs or reclaimed (**Difference between boxes 3 and 4**)	Box 5	21,456.07
Total value of **sales** and all other outputs excluding any VAT. **Include your box 8 figure**	Box 6	268,199
Total value of purchases and all other inputs excluding any VAT. **Include your box 9 figure**	Box 7	111,811
Total value of all **supplies** of goods and related costs, excluding any VAT, to other **EU Member States**	Box 8	43,789
Total value of all **acquisitions** of goods and related costs, excluding any VAT, from other **EU Member States**	Box 9	15,390

Workings

Box 1

	£
VAT on UK sales	37,293.60
VAT on EU sales (to non-registered customers)	2,200.00
Add: Output VAT error (£10,500 × 20%)	2,100.00
Box 1 total	41,593.60

Box 2

(£15,390 × 20%)	3,078.00

Box 4

Purchases (UK standard-rated)	19,284.20
Acquisitions (EU) (£15,390 × 20%)	3,078.00
Add: VAT reclaimed on bad debt	853.33
	23,215.53

Box 6

UK sales	213,410
EU sales	54,789
	268,199

Box 7

UK purchases	96,421
EU purchases	15,390
	111,811

Task 8

(a)

Email
To: Financial accountant
From: Junior accountant
Date: 15.1.X1
Subject: VAT return
Please be advised that I have just completed the VAT return for the quarter ended (………**31.12.X0**………………).
The return must be filed by (…………**7 February 20X1…..**).
The amount of VAT **(receivable)** will be ….**£16,520.44**
This will be **received directly into our bank account.**
Kind regards

(b)   The correct answer is A.

B and C would be ethically acceptable courses of action.

Accounting Qualification

Indirect Tax IDRX (Level 3)
Reference material

Finance Act 2018 – for assessment 1 January – 31 December 2019

The Association of Accounting Technicians

Reference material for AAT assessment of Indirect Tax

Introduction

This document comprises data that you may need to consult during your Indirect Tax computer-based assessment.

The material can be consulted during the sample and live assessments through pop-up windows. It is made available here so you can familiarise yourself with the content before the test.

Do not take a print of this document into the exam room with you*.

This document may be changed to reflect periodical updates in the computer-based assessment, so please check you have the most recent version while studying. This version is based on Finance Act 2018 and is for use in AAT assessments 1 January – 31 December 2019.

*Unless you need a printed version as part of reasonable adjustments for particular needs, in which case you must discuss this with your tutor at least six weeks before the assessment date.

Introduction to VAT

VAT is a tax that's charged on most goods and services that VAT-registered businesses provide in the UK. It's also charged on goods and some services that are imported from countries outside the European Union (EU), and brought into the UK from other EU countries.

VAT is charged when a VAT-registered business sells taxable goods and services to either another business or to a non-business customer. This is called output tax.

When a VAT-registered business buys taxable goods or services for business use it can generally reclaim the VAT it has paid. This is called input tax.

Her Majesty's Revenue and Customs (HMRC) is the government department responsible for operating the VAT system. Payments of VAT collected are made by VAT-registered businesses to HMRC.

Rates of VAT

There are three rates of VAT, depending on the goods or services the business provides. The rates are:
- standard – 20%. The standard-rate VAT fraction for calculating the VAT element of a gross supply is 20/120 or 1/6
- reduced – 5%.
- zero – 0%

There are also some goods and services that are:
- exempt from VAT
- outside the scope of VAT (outside the UK VAT system altogether)

Taxable supplies

Zero-rated goods and services count as taxable supplies and are part of taxable turnover, but no VAT is added to the selling price because the VAT rate is 0%.

If the business sells goods and services that are exempt, no VAT is added as they're not taxable supplies and they're also not taxable turnover.

Generally, a business can't register for VAT or reclaim the VAT on purchases if it only sells exempt goods and services. Where some of its supplies are of exempt goods and services, the business is referred to as partially exempt. It may not be able to reclaim the VAT on all of its purchases.

A business which buys and sells only - or mainly - zero-rated goods or services can apply to HMRC to be exempt from registering for VAT. This could make sense if the business pays little or no VAT on purchases.

Taxable turnover

Taxable turnover consists of standard-rated sales plus all reduced-rated and zero-rated sales but excludes the VAT on those sales, exempt sales and out-of-scope sales. If one VAT-registered business acquires another business it immediately absorbs the turnover of that business, whether the acquired business is registered for VAT or not. All VAT decisions must thereafter be made based on the combined turnover.

Change in VAT rate

Generally a business must use the VAT rate applicable from the time of the legislative change, unless payment has already been received or the goods have already been delivered. In these cases a tax point has already been created and the rate applicable will have been set by the tax point.

An exception arises where the goods have been delivered, or otherwise removed by the customer, the supplier has elected to follow the 14-day rule for issuing VAT invoices and the VAT rate increases between the date of delivery of the goods and the issuing of the invoice. In this case it is the new VAT rate which applies.

Immediately after the rate change a business may opt to honour supplies of goods and services at the rate which applied when the contract to supply was agreed, however output tax is still accountable at the new rate.

If the business offers a prompt payment discount and opts to issue a credit note to cover the reduction in payment made by the customer then a change in VAT rate which occurs between the issue of the original invoice and final payment will not be affected by the change in VAT rate. The rate due on the credit note, issued to account for the reduced payment made, will be fixed by the tax point of the original invoice.

Registration and deregistration

Registration threshold

If, as at the end of any month, taxable turnover for the previous 12 months is more than the current registration threshold of £85,000, the business must register for VAT within 30 days. Registration without delay is required if, at any time, the value of taxable turnover in the next 30 day period alone is expected to be more than the registration threshold.

A business which has trading that temporarily takes it above the VAT threshold of £85,000 but which expects turnover to drop back below the threshold almost immediately can apply to stay unregistered, but the business must be able to prove to HMRC that the momentary increase is a true one-off occurrence.

If trading is below the registration threshold

If taxable turnover hasn't crossed the registration threshold, the business can still apply to register for VAT voluntarily.

Deregistration threshold

The deregistration threshold is £83,000. If taxable turnover for the previous 12 months is less than or equal to £83,000, or if it is expected to fall to £83,000 or less in the next 12 months, the business can either:
- voluntarily remain registered for VAT, or
- ask HMRC for its VAT registration to be cancelled

Failure to register

A business which fails to register when it is required to do so may face a civil penalty. More importantly HMRC will treat the business as though it had registered on time and will expect VAT to be accounted for as if it had been charged. The business has two choices in respect of this VAT, which it has not included in its invoices.

It may either:

- Allow HMRC to treat the invoices as VAT inclusive and absorb the VAT which should have been charged, OR
- Account for VAT as an addition to the charges already invoiced and attempt to recover this VAT from its customers.

Cancellation of VAT registration

A registration must be cancelled if the business is closed down or ceases to make taxable supplies.

If a business is being taken over by a business with a completely different structure, for example an unincorporated business being taken over by an incorporated business or vice versa, the original registration must be cancelled. It will either be replaced by a new registration for the new business, or be subsumed into the registration of the expanded business. In some circumstances the new business may apply for the registration of the business being taken over to be re-allocated to the new business. This may happen because two businesses merge and only one is currently registered. Re-allocation of the existing registration may be the most appropriate method of dealing with VAT registration.

Changes to the VAT registration

Some business changes will necessitate a change in details of the VAT registration, such as a change in the trading name or the address of the business. Other reasons for changes to the registration are a change in main business activities, particularly if this means a significant change to the types of supply, and changes to the business bank account details.

Failure to notify HMRC of changes which either cancel or change registration within 30 days of the relevant change may render the business and its owners liable to a civil penalty.

Keeping business records and VAT records

All VAT-registered businesses must keep certain business and VAT records.

These records are not required to be kept in a set way, provided they:
- are complete and up to date
- allow the correct amount of VAT owed to HMRC or by HMRC to be worked out
- are easily accessible when an HMRC visit takes place, eg the figures used to fill in the VAT Return must be easy to find

Business records

Business records which must be kept include the following:
- annual accounts, including statements of profit or loss
- bank statements and paying-in slips
- cash books and other account books
- orders and delivery notes
- purchases and sales day books
- records of daily takings such as till rolls
- relevant business correspondence

VAT records

In addition to these business records, VAT records must be kept.

In general, the business must keep the following VAT records:
- Records of all the standard-rated, reduced-rated, zero-rated and exempt goods and services that are bought and sold.
- Copies of all sales invoices issued. However, businesses do not have to keep copies of any less detailed (simplified) VAT invoices for items under £250 including VAT
- All purchase invoices for items purchased for business purposes unless the gross value of the supply is £25 or less and the purchase was from a coin-operated telephone or vending machine, or for car parking charges or tolls.
- All credit notes and debit notes received.
- Copies of all credit notes and debit notes issued.
- Records of any goods or services bought for which there is no VAT reclaim, such as business entertainment.
- Records of any goods exported.
- Any adjustments, such as corrections to the accounts or amended VAT invoices.

Generally all business records that are relevant for VAT must be kept for at least six years. If this causes serious problems in terms of storage or costs, then HMRC may allow some records to be kept for a shorter period. Records may be stored digitally especially if that is needed to overcome storage and access difficulties.

Keeping a VAT account

A VAT account is the separate record that must be kept of the VAT charged on taxable sales (referred to as output tax or VAT payable) and the VAT paid on purchases (called input tax or VAT reclaimable). It provides the link between the business records and the VAT Return. A VAT-registered business needs to add up the VAT in the sales and purchases records and then transfer these totals to the VAT account, using separate headings for VAT payable and VAT reclaimable.

The VAT account can be kept in whatever way suits the business best, as long as it includes information about the VAT that it:
- owes on sales, including when fuel scale charges are used
- owes on acquisitions from other European Union (EU) countries
- owes following a correction or error adjustment
- can reclaim on business purchases
- can reclaim on acquisitions from other EU countries
- can reclaim following a correction or error adjustment
- is reclaiming via VAT bad debt relief

The business must also keep records of any adjustments that have been made, such as balancing payments for the annual accounting scheme for VAT.

Information from the VAT account can be used to complete the VAT Return at the end of each accounting period. VAT reclaimable is subtracted from the VAT payable, to give the net amount of VAT to pay to or reclaim from HMRC.

Unless it is using the cash accounting scheme, a business:
- must pay the VAT charged on invoices to customers during the accounting period that relates to the return, even if those customers have not paid the invoices
- may reclaim the VAT charged on invoices from suppliers during the accounting period that relates to the return, even if it has not paid the invoices.

Exempt and partly-exempt businesses

Exempt goods and services

There are some goods and services on which VAT is not charged.

Exempt supplies are not taxable for VAT, so sales of exempt goods and services are not included in taxable turnover for VAT purposes. If a registered business buys exempt items, there is no VAT to reclaim.

(This is different to zero-rated supplies. In both cases VAT is not added to the selling price, but zero-rated goods or services are taxable for VAT at 0%, and are included in taxable turnover.)

Businesses which only sell or supply exempt goods or services

A business which only supplies goods or services that are exempt from VAT is called an exempt business. It cannot register for VAT, so it won't be able to reclaim any input tax on business purchases.

(Again this is different to zero-rated supplies, as a business can reclaim the input tax on any purchases that relate to zero-rated sales. In addition, a business which sells mainly or only zero-rated items may apply for an exemption from VAT registration, but then it can't claim back any input tax.)

Reclaiming VAT in a partly-exempt business

A business that is registered for VAT but that makes some exempt supplies is referred to as partly, or partially, exempt.

Generally, such businesses won't be able to reclaim the input tax paid on purchases that relate to exempt supplies.

However if the amount of input tax incurred relating to exempt supplies is below a minimum 'de minimus' amount, input tax can be reclaimed in full.

If the amount of input tax incurred relating to exempt supplies is above the 'de minimus' amount, only the part of the input tax that related to non-exempt supplies can be reclaimed.

Place of supply

Businesses which make supplies of goods and services to other member states of the EU or to countries outside the EU, or which receive goods and services from other member states of the EU or from countries outside the EU, must apply the "place of supply" rules for both goods and services. Place of supply is important because it drives the amount of VAT, if any, which is to be added to the cost of the services, and the manner in which any VAT is accounted for.

The place of supply is the place, or country, where the supply is made.

The following rules apply to a supplier based in the UK, with no alternative location elsewhere in the EU or outside the EU.

Supplies and receipts of goods

The place of supply for goods is always the country where the goods originate. This applies whether the goods are for the enjoyment of a business customer or a domestic customer.

Supplies and receipts of services

Supplies of services are covered by the "Place of supply of services order" or POSSO. Here the place of supply can be different depending on who the customer is, and whether the supply of services is within, or outside, the EU.

When the customer is a business customer the place of supply is where the customer is.

Should the customer be either:
- a non-business,
- an unregistered business, or
- a registered business, but the supply is of a non-business nature

then the place of supply is the country where the supplier is, irrespective of where the customer is.

Tax points

The time of supply, known as the 'tax point', is the date when a transaction takes place for VAT purposes. This date is not necessarily the date the supply physically takes place.

Generally, a registered business must pay or reclaim VAT in the (usually quarterly) VAT period, or tax period, in which the time of supply occurs, and it must use the correct rate of VAT in force on that date. This means knowing the time of supply/tax point for every transaction is important, as it must be put on the right VAT Return.

Time of supply (tax point) for goods and services

The time of supply for VAT purposes is defined as follows.
- For transactions where no VAT invoice is issued, the time of supply is normally the date the supply takes place (as defined below).
- For transactions where there is a VAT invoice, the time of supply is normally the date the invoice is issued, even if this is after the date the supply took place (as defined below).

To issue a VAT invoice, it must be sent (by post, email etc) or given to the customer for them to keep. A tax point cannot be created simply by preparing an invoice.

However there are exceptions to these rules on time of supply, detailed below.

Date the supply takes place

For goods, the time when the goods are considered to be supplied for VAT purposes is the date when one of the following happens.
- The supplier sends the goods to the customer.
- The customer collects the goods from the supplier.
- The goods (which are not either sent or collected) are made available for the customer to use, for example if the supplier is assembling something on the customer's premises.

For services, the date when the services are supplied for VAT purposes is the date when the service is carried out and all the work - except invoicing - is finished.

Exceptions regarding time of supply (tax point)

The above general principles for working out the time of supply do not apply in the following situations.

- For transactions where a VAT invoice is issued, or payment is received, in advance of the date of supply, the time of supply is the date the invoice is issued or the payment is received, whichever is the earlier.

- If the supplier receives full payment before the date when the supply takes place and no VAT invoice has yet been issued, the time of supply is the date the payment is received.

- If the supplier receives part-payment before the date when the supply takes place, the time of supply becomes the date the part-payment is received but only for the amount of the part-payment (assuming no VAT invoice has been issued before this date - in which case the time of supply is the date the invoice is issued). The time of supply for the remainder will follow the normal rules - and might fall in a different VAT period, and so have to go onto a different VAT Return.

- If the supplier issues a VAT invoice more than 14 days after the date when the supply took place, the time of supply will be the date the supply took place, and not the date the invoice is issued. However, if a supplier has genuine commercial difficulties in invoicing within 14 days of the supply taking place, they can contact HMRC to ask for permission to issue invoices later than 14 days and move the time of supply to this later date.

- Where services are being supplied on a continuous basis over a period in excess of a month but invoices are being issued regularly throughout the period. A tax point is created every time an invoice is issued or a payment is made, whichever happens first. A business may issue invoices for a whole 12 month period but only if it is known that payments will be made regularly.

- Goods supplied to a customer on a sale or return basis remain the property of the supplier until the customer indicates they are intending to keep them. If a time limit has been fixed for the sale or return the tax point is:

    o Where the fixed period is 12 months or less – the date the time limit expires
    o Where the fixed period is more than 12 months, or there is no fixed period – 12 months from the date the goods were sent
    o Where the customer adopts the goods before the fixed period has expired – the date the goods are adopted.

A payment made, which is not returnable, normally indicates that the goods have been adopted, however the receipt of a deposit which is repayable if the goods are returned is not an indication of adoption.

VAT invoices

To whom is a VAT invoice issued?

Whenever a VAT-registered business supplies taxable goods or services to another VAT-registered business, it must give the customer a VAT invoice.

A VAT-registered business is not required to issue a VAT invoice to a non-registered business or to a member of the public, but it must do so if requested.

What is a VAT invoice?

A VAT invoice shows certain VAT details of a supply of goods or services. It can be either in paper or electronic form. An electronic invoice (e-invoice) is only valid if it is in a secure format, for example a "pdf".

A VAT-registered customer must have a valid VAT invoice from the supplier in order to claim back the VAT they have paid on the purchase for their business.

What is NOT a VAT invoice?

The following are NOT VAT invoices:
- pro-forma invoices
- invoices for only zero-rated or exempt supplies
- invoices that state 'this is not a VAT invoice'
- statements of account
- delivery notes
- orders
- letters, emails or other correspondence

A registered business cannot reclaim the VAT it has paid on a purchase by using these documents as proof of payment.

What a VAT invoice must show

A VAT invoice must show:
- an invoice number which is unique and follows on from the number of the previous invoice - any spoiled or cancelled serially numbered invoice must be kept to show to a VAT officer at the next VAT inspection
- the seller's name or trading name, and address
- the seller's VAT registration number
- the invoice date
- the time of supply or tax point if this is different from the invoice date
- the customer's name or trading name, and address
- a description sufficient to identify the goods or services supplied to the customer

For each different type of item listed on the invoice, the business must show:
- the unit price or rate, excluding VAT
- the quantity of goods or the extent of the services
- the rate of VAT that applies to what is being sold
- the total amount payable, excluding VAT
- the rate of any cash or settlement discount
- the total amount of VAT charged

If the business issues a VAT invoice that includes zero-rated or exempt goods or services, it must:
- show clearly that there is no VAT payable on those goods or services
- show the total of those values separately

Where a prompt payment discount (PPD) is offered VAT must be accounted for to HMRC on the actual consideration received. The business must decide how to express this on the invoice. It may:
- invoice at the discounted value with VAT on that amount and then issue an additional invoice for the discount plus VAT at the point it becomes clear the customer will not take the discount by paying within the prompt payment period, OR
- invoice for the full value with VAT on that amount and then issue a credit note for the discount plus VAT should the customer pay the discounted value within the prompt payment period, OR
- invoice for the full value of the supply and associated VAT but provide information to the customer which allows it to determine how much to pay if they make payment within the prompt payment discount period. This information must include details of the input tax which they are permitted to recover depending on when they make payment. A warning should be included to the customer that failure to account for the correct amount of VAT is an offence.

Rounding on VAT invoices

The total VAT payable on all goods and services shown on a VAT invoice may be rounded down to a whole penny. Any fraction of a penny can be ignored. (This concession is not available to retailers.)

Time limits for issuing VAT invoices

There is a strict time limit on issuing VAT invoices. Normally a VAT invoice to a VAT-registered customer must be issued within 30 days of the basic tax point, which is either the date of supply of the goods or services, subject to the 14 day rule or, if the business was paid in advance, the date payment was received. This is so the customer can claim back the VAT on the supply, if they are entitled to do so.

The 30 day limit for goods starts with the day the goods are sent to the customer or taken by the customer or made available to the customer.

Invoices cannot be issued any later without permission from HMRC, except in a few limited circumstances.

A valid VAT invoice is needed to reclaim VAT

Even if a business is registered for VAT, it can normally only reclaim VAT on purchases if:
- they are for use in the business or for business purposes and
- a valid VAT invoice for the purchase is received and retained*.

*Subject to the rules for VAT invoices for supplies of £250 or less including VAT and for supplies of £25 including VAT or less:
- A simplified invoice for supplies of £250 or less is acceptable as a "valid VAT invoice" for input tax reclaim.
- Supplies of £25 or less including VAT, supported by a simple till receipt, can be assumed to be acceptable as a "valid VAT invoice" for input tax reclaim as long as the business has a reasonable understanding that the supplier is VAT registered.

Only VAT-registered businesses can issue valid VAT invoices. A business cannot reclaim VAT on any goods or services that are purchased from a business that is not VAT-registered.

Where simplified (less detailed) VAT invoices can be issued

Simplified VAT invoices

If a VAT-registered business makes taxable supplies of goods or services for £250 or less including VAT, then it can issue a simplified (less detailed) VAT invoice that only needs to show:
- the seller's name and address
- the seller's VAT registration number
- the time of supply (tax point)
- a description of the goods or services
- the total payable including VAT

If the supply includes items at different VAT rates then, for each different VAT rate, the simplified VAT invoice must also show the VAT rate applicable to the item(s).

Exempt supplies must not be included on a simplified VAT invoice.

There is no requirement for the business making the supply to keep copies of any less detailed invoices it has issued.

Pro-forma invoices

If there is a need to issue a sales document for goods or services not supplied yet, the business can issue a 'pro-forma' invoice or a similar document as part of the offer to supply goods or services to customers.

A pro-forma invoice is not a VAT invoice, and it should be clearly marked with the words "This is not a VAT invoice".

If a potential customer accepts the goods or services offered to them and these are actually supplied, then a VAT invoice must be issued within the appropriate time limit if appropriate.

If the business has been issued with a pro-forma invoice by a supplier it cannot be used to claim back VAT on the purchase. A VAT invoice must be obtained from the supplier.

Advance payments or deposits

An advance payment, or deposit, is a proportion of the total selling price that a customer pays before they are supplied with goods or services. When a business asks for an advance payment or deposit, the tax point is whichever of the following happens first:
- the date a VAT invoice is issued for the advance payment
- the date the advance payment is received

The business must include the VAT on the advance payment or deposit on the VAT Return for the period when the tax point occurs.

If the customer pays any remaining balance before the goods are delivered or the services are performed, another tax point is created when whichever of the following happens first:
- a VAT invoice is issued for the balance
- payment of the balance is received

The VAT on the balance must be included on the VAT Return for the period when the tax point occurs.

VAT does not have to be accounted for if a deposit is either:
- Refunded to the customer in full when they return goods safely, or
- Kept as compensation for loss of or damage to the goods.

Discounts on goods and services

If any goods or services supplied by a VAT-registered business are subject to a trade, bulk or other form of discount, VAT is charged on the VAT invoice on the discounted price rather than the full price.

Returned goods, credit notes, debit notes and VAT

For a buyer who has received a VAT invoice

If goods are returned to the seller for full or partial credit there are three options:
- return the invoice to the supplier and obtain a replacement invoice showing the proper amount of VAT due, if any
- obtain a credit note from the supplier
- issue a debit note to the supplier

If the buyer issues a debit note or receives a credit note, it must:
- record this in the accounting records
- enter it on the next VAT Return, deducting the VAT on the credit or debit note from the amount of VAT which can be reclaimed

For a seller who has issued a VAT invoice

If goods are returned by a customer, there are again three options:
- cancel and recover the original invoice, and issue a replacement showing the correct amount of any VAT due, if any
- issue a credit note to the customer
- obtain a debit note from the customer

If the seller issues a credit note or receives a debit note, it must:
- record this in the accounting records
- enter it on the next VAT Return, deducting the VAT on the credit or debit note from the amount of VAT payable

Entertainment expenses

Business entertainment

Business entertainment is any form of free or subsidised entertainment or hospitality to non-employees, for example suppliers and customers. Generally a business cannot reclaim input tax on business entertainment expenses. The exception is that input tax can be reclaimed in respect of entertaining overseas customers, but not UK or Isle of Man customers.

Employee expenses and entertainment

The business can, however, reclaim VAT on employee expenses and employee entertainment expenses if those expenses relate to travel and subsistence or where the entertainment applies only to employees.

When the entertainment is in respect of a mixed group of both employees and non-employees (eg customers and/or suppliers), the business can only reclaim VAT on the proportion of the expenses that is for employees and on the proportion for overseas customers.

Vehicles and motoring expenses

VAT and vehicles

When it buys a car a registered business generally cannot reclaim the VAT. There are some exceptions - for example, when the car is used mainly as one of the following:
- a taxi
- for driving instruction
- for self-drive hire

If the VAT on the original purchase price of a car bought new is not reclaimed, the business does not have to charge any VAT when it is sold. This is because the sale of the car is exempt for VAT purposes. If the business did reclaim the VAT when it bought the car new, VAT is chargeable when it comes to sell it.

VAT-registered businesses can generally reclaim the VAT when they buy a commercial vehicle such as a van, lorry or tractor.

Reclaiming VAT on road fuel

If the business pays for road fuel, it can deal with the VAT charged on the fuel in one of four ways:
- Reclaim all of the VAT. All of the fuel must be used only for business purposes.
- Reclaim all of the VAT and pay the appropriate fuel scale charge - this is a way of accounting for output tax on fuel that the business buys but that is then used for private motoring.
- Reclaim only the VAT that relates to fuel used for business mileage. Detailed records of business and private mileage must be kept.
- Do not reclaim any VAT. This can be a useful option if mileage is low and also if fuel is used for both business and private motoring. If the business chooses this option it must apply it to all vehicles, including commercial vehicles.

Transactions outside the UK

Exports, despatches and supplying goods abroad: charging VAT

If a business sells, supplies or transfers goods out of the UK to someone in another country it may need to charge VAT on them.

VAT on exports of goods to non-EU countries

Generally speaking, the business can zero-rate supplies exported outside the EU, provided it follows strict rules, obtains and keeps the necessary evidence, and obeys all laws.

The term 'exports' is reserved to describe sales to a country outside the EU. Goods supplied to another EU member state are technically known as despatches rather than exports.

VAT on despatches of goods to someone who is not VAT registered in another EU member state

When a business supplies goods to someone in another EU member state, and they are not registered for VAT in that country, it should normally charge VAT.

VAT on despatches of goods to someone who is VAT registered in another EU member state

If, however, goods are supplied to someone who is registered for VAT in the destination EU member state, the business can zero-rate the supply for VAT purposes, provided it meets certain conditions.

Imports, acquisitions and purchasing goods from abroad: paying and reclaiming VAT

Generally speaking, VAT is payable on all purchases of goods that are bought from abroad at the same rate that would apply to the goods if bought in the UK. The business must tell HMRC about goods that it imports, and pay any VAT and duty that is due.

VAT on imports of goods from non-EU countries

VAT may be charged on imports of goods bought from non-EU countries. The business can reclaim any VAT paid on the goods imported as input tax.

VAT on goods acquired from EU member states

If a business is registered for VAT in the UK and buys goods from inside the EU, these are known as acquisitions rather than imports. Usually no VAT is charged by the supplier but acquisition tax, at the same rate of VAT that would apply if the goods were supplied in the UK, is due on the acquisition. This is included in Box 2 of the VAT return. It can be reclaimed as input tax in Box 4 of the VAT return as if the goods were bought in the UK.

Bad debts

When a business can reclaim VAT on bad debts

VAT that has been paid to HMRC and which has not been received from the customer can be reclaimed as bad debt relief. The conditions are that:

- the debt is more than six months and less than four years and six months old
- the debt has been written off in the VAT account and transferred to a separate bad debt account
- the debt has not been sold or handed to a factoring company
- the business did not charge more than the normal selling price for the items

Bad debt relief does not apply when the cash accounting scheme is used because the VAT is not paid to HMRC until after the customer has paid it to the supplier.

How to claim bad debt relief

If the business is entitled to claim bad debt relief, add the amount of VAT to be reclaimed to the amount of VAT being reclaimed on purchases (input tax) and put the total figure in Box 4 of the VAT Return.

Effect of a change in the business

If a business closes down, relief for all outstanding bad debts up to and including the date of closure will need to be claimed, if eligible.

Where a business is acquired as a going concern and the acquiring business takes on the VAT registration of the closing business, it may be possible to transfer the outstanding bad debts from the old to the new business.

Completing the online VAT Return, box by box

The online VAT Return is completed as follows:

Box 1 – VAT due in this period on sales and other outputs

- This is the total amount of VAT charged on sales to customers. It also has to include VAT due to HMRC for other reasons, for example fuel scale charges.
- Include VAT due on a supply of services from another member state of the EC, where the supplier has "zero-rated" the supply.

Box 2 – VAT due in this period on acquisitions from other EC Member States

- VAT due, but not yet paid, on goods bought from other EU member states, and any services directly related to those goods (such as delivery charges). The business may be able to reclaim this amount, and if so it must be included in the total in Box 4.

Box 3 – Total VAT due (the sum of boxes 1 and 2). This is calculated automatically by the online return

Box 4 – VAT reclaimed in this period on purchases and other inputs (including acquisitions from the EC)

- This is the VAT charged on purchases for use in the business. It should also include:
  o VAT paid on imports from countries outside the EC
  o VAT due (but not yet paid) on goods from other EC member states, and any services directly related to those goods (such as delivery charges) - this is the figure in Box 2.
  o VAT due on a supply of services from a supplier in another member state of the EC where that supply has been "zero-rated" by the supplier. This will be the same amount as entered in Box 1 in respect of the same transaction.

Box 5 – Net VAT to be paid to HM Revenue & Customs or reclaimed by you (Difference between boxes 3 and 4). This is calculated automatically by the online return

Box 6 – Total value of sales and all other outputs excluding any VAT. Include your box 8 figure.

- Enter the total figure for sales (excluding VAT) for the period, that is the sales on which the VAT entered in Box 1 was based. Additionally, also include:
  o any zero-rated and exempt sales or other supplies made
  o any amount entered in Box 8
  o exports to outside the EC.

  The net amount of any credit notes issued, or debit notes received, is deducted.

Box 7 – Total value of purchases and all other inputs excluding any VAT. Include your box 9 figure.

- Enter the total figure for purchases (excluding VAT) for the period, that is the purchases on which the VAT entered in Box 4 was based. Additionally, also include:
  o any zero-rated and exempt purchases
  o any amount entered in Box 9
  o imports from outside the EU.

Box 8 – Total value of all supplies of goods and related costs, excluding any VAT, to other EC Member States.

- Enter the total value of goods supplied to another EC member state and services related to those goods (such as delivery charges).

Box 9 – Total value of all acquisitions of goods and related costs, excluding any VAT, from other EC Member States.

- Enter the total value of goods received from VAT registered suppliers in another EC member state and services related to those goods (such as delivery charges).

VAT periods, submitting returns and paying VAT

VAT Returns for transactions to the end of the relevant VAT period must be submitted by the due date shown on the VAT Return. VAT due must also be paid by the due date.

What is a VAT period?

A VAT period is the period of time over which the business records VAT transactions in the VAT account for completion of the VAT Return. The VAT period is three months (a quarter) unless the annual accounting scheme is used. The end dates of a business's four VAT periods are determined when it first registers for VAT, but it can choose to amend the dates on which its VAT periods end. This is often done to match VAT periods to accounting period ends.

Submitting VAT Returns online and paying HMRC electronically

It is mandatory for virtually all VAT-registered traders to submit their VAT Returns to HMRC using online filing, and to pay HMRC electronically.

Due dates for submitting the VAT Return and paying electronically

Businesses are responsible for calculating how much VAT they owe and for paying VAT so that the amount clears to HMRC's bank account on or before the due date. Paying on time avoids having to pay a surcharge for late payment.

The normal due date for submitting each VAT Return and electronically paying HMRC any VAT that is owed is one calendar month after the end of the relevant VAT period, unless the annual accounting scheme is operated. The normal due date for the return and payment can be found on the return.

Online filing and electronic payment mean that businesses get an extended due date for filing the return of seven extra calendar days after the normal due date shown on the VAT Return. This extra seven days also applies to paying HMRC so that the amount has cleared into HMRC's bank account. However this does not apply if the business uses the Annual Accounting Scheme for VAT.

If the business pays HMRC by Direct Debit, HMRC automatically collects payment from the business's bank account three bank working days after the extra seven calendar days following the normal due date.

If the business fails to pay cleared funds into HMRC's bank account by the payment deadline, or fails to have sufficient funds in its account to meet the direct debit, it may be liable to a surcharge for late payment.

Repayment of VAT

If the amount of VAT reclaimed (entered in Box 4) is more than the VAT to be paid (entered in Box 3), then the net VAT value in Box 5 is a repayment due to the business from HMRC.

HMRC is obliged to schedule this sum for repayment automatically, provided checks applied to the VAT Return do not indicate that such a repayment might not be due. There may be circumstances when the business does not receive the repayment automatically, for instance if there is an outstanding debt owed to HMRC.

Special accounting schemes

Annual Accounting Scheme for VAT

Using standard VAT accounting, four VAT Returns each year are required. Any VAT due is payable quarterly, and any VAT refunds due are also receivable quarterly.

Using the normal annual accounting scheme, the business makes nine interim payments at monthly intervals. There is only one VAT Return to complete, at the end of the year, when either a balancing payment is payable or a balancing refund is receivable.

Businesses can start on the annual accounting scheme if their estimated taxable turnover during the next tax year is not more than £1.35 million. Businesses already using the annual accounting scheme can continue to do so until the estimated taxable turnover for the next tax year exceeds £1.6 million. If the business is taken over as a going concern the acquiring business must assess the use of the annual accounting scheme in the context of the expected and combined turnover of the new business, and must immediately cease using the scheme if that is expected to exceed £1.6m.

Whilst using the annual accounting scheme the business may also be able to use either the cash accounting scheme or the flat rate scheme, but not both.

Benefits of annual accounting

- One VAT Return per year, instead of four.
- Two months after the tax period end to complete and send in the annual VAT Return and pay the balance of VAT payable, rather than the usual one month.
- Better management of cash flow by paying a fixed amount in nine instalments.
- Ability to make additional payments as and when required.
- Join from VAT registration day, or at any other time if already registered for VAT.

Disadvantages of annual accounting

- Only one repayment per year, which is not beneficial if the business regularly requires refunds.
- If turnover decreases, interim payments may be higher than the VAT payments would be under standard VAT accounting – again there is a need to wait until the end of the year to receive a refund.

Cash Accounting Scheme for VAT

Using standard VAT accounting, VAT is paid on sales within a VAT period whether or not the customer has paid. VAT is reclaimed on purchases whether or not the business has paid the supplier.

Using cash accounting, VAT is not paid until the customer has paid the invoice. If a customer never pays, the business never has to pay the VAT. VAT is reclaimed on purchases only when the business has paid the invoice.

Cash accounting can be used if the estimated taxable turnover during the next tax year is not more than £1.35 million. A business can continue to use cash accounting until its taxable turnover exceeds £1.6 million.

The cash accounting scheme may be used in conjunction with the annual accounting scheme but not with the flat rate scheme. If the business is taken over as a going concern the acquiring business must assess the use of the cash accounting scheme in the context of the expected and combined turnover of the new business, and must immediately cease using the scheme if that is expected to exceed £1.6m.

Benefits of cash accounting

Using cash accounting may help cash flow, especially if customers are slow payers. Payment of VAT is not made until the business has received payment from the customer, so if a customer never pays, VAT does not have to be paid on that bad debt as long as the business is using the cash accounting scheme.

Disadvantages of cash accounting

Using cash accounting may adversely affect cash flow:
- The business cannot reclaim VAT on purchases until it has paid for them. This can be a disadvantage if most goods and services are purchased on credit.
- Businesses which regularly reclaim more VAT than they pay will usually receive repayment later under cash accounting than under standard VAT accounting, unless they pay for everything at the time of purchase.
- If a business starts using cash accounting when it starts trading, it will not be able to reclaim VAT on most start-up expenditure, such as initial stock, tools or machinery, until it has actually paid for those items.
- When it leaves the cash accounting scheme the business will have to account for all outstanding VAT due, including on any bad debts.

Flat Rate Scheme for VAT

If its VAT-exclusive taxable turnover is less than £150,000 per year, the business could simplify its VAT accounting by registering on the Flat Rate Scheme and calculating VAT payments as a percentage of its total VAT-inclusive turnover. There is no reclaim of VAT on purchases - this is taken into account in calculating the flat rate percentage that applies to the business.

The VAT flat rate the business uses usually depends on its business type. It may pay a different rate if it only spends a small amount on goods.

Limited cost business

The business is classed as a 'limited cost business' if its goods cost less than either:
- 2% of its turnover
- £1,000 a year (if its costs are more than 2%)

This means the business pays a flat rate of 16.5%, whatever its business type.

Non-limited cost businesses use their business type to determine the applicable flat rate.

Reclaim of VAT on capital expenditure goods

If the business uses the Flat Rate Scheme, it can reclaim the VAT it has been charged on a single purchase of capital expenditure goods where the amount of the purchase, including VAT, is £2,000 or more.

These capital expenditure goods are dealt with outside the Flat Rate Scheme. This means that the input tax is claimed in box 4 of the VAT return. If the supply is:
- more than one purchase
- under £2,000 including VAT, or

- of services

then no VAT is claimable, as this input tax is already taken into account in the calculation of the flat rate percentage.

The flat rate scheme can reduce the time needed in accounting for and working out VAT. Even though the business still needs to show a VAT amount on each VAT invoice issued, it does not need to record how much VAT it charged on every sale in its ledger accounts. Nor does it need to record the VAT paid on every purchase.

Once on the scheme, the business can continue to use it until its total business income exceeds £230,000. If the business is taken over as a going concern the acquiring business must assess the use of the flat rate scheme in the context of the expected and combined turnover of the new business, and must immediately cease using the scheme if that is expected to exceed £230,000. The flat rate scheme may be used in conjunction with the annual accounting scheme but not the cash accounting scheme.

Benefits of using the flat rate scheme

Using the flat rate scheme can save time and smooth cash flow. It offers these benefits:
- No need to record the VAT charged on every sale and purchase, as with standard VAT accounting. This can save time. But although the business only has to pay HMRC a percentage of its turnover, it must still show VAT at the appropriate normal rate (standard, reduced or zero) on the VAT invoices it issues.
- A first year discount. A business in its first year of VAT registration gets a 1% reduction in the applicable flat rate percentage until the day before the first anniversary of VAT registration.
- Fewer rules to follow, for instance no longer having to work out what VAT on purchases can or cannot be reclaimed.
- Peace of mind, less chance of mistakes and fewer worries about getting the VAT right.
- Certainty. The business always knows what percentage of takings has to be paid to HMRC.

Potential disadvantages of using the flat rate scheme

The flat rate percentages are calculated in a way that takes into account zero-rated and exempt sales. They also contain an allowance for the VAT spent on purchases. So the VAT Flat Rate Scheme might not be right for the business if:
- it buys mostly standard-rated items, as there is no reclaim of any VAT on purchases
- it regularly receives a VAT repayment under standard VAT accounting
- it makes a lot of zero-rated or exempt sales.
- It is a 'limited cost business'

Errors in previous VAT Returns

Action to be taken at the end of the VAT period

At the end of the VAT period, the business should calculate the net value of all the errors and omissions found during the period that relate to VAT Returns already submitted - that is, any tax which should have been claimed back is subtracted from any additional tax due to HMRC, and any tax that should have been paid is added. Any deliberate errors must not be included - these must be separately declared to HMRC.

What the business should do next depends on whether the net value of all the errors is less than or greater than the 'error correction reporting threshold', which is the greater of:
- £10,000
- 1% of the box 6 figure on the VAT Return for the period when the error was discovered - subject to an upper limit of £50,000

If the net value of all the errors is less than the error reporting threshold then, if preferred, the errors may be corrected by making an adjustment on the current VAT Return (Method 1).

However, if the value of the net VAT error discovered is above this threshold, it must be declared to HMRC separately, in writing (Method 2).

How to adjust the VAT Return: Method 1

Errors from previous VAT Returns can be corrected by adjusting the VAT amounts on the current VAT Return.

At the end of the VAT period when the errors are discovered, the VAT account of output tax due or input tax claimed is adjusted by the net amount of all errors. The VAT account must show the amount of the adjustment being made to the VAT Return.

If more than one error is discovered in the same exercise, the net value of all the errors is used to adjust the VAT liability on the VAT Return.

Either Box 1 or Box 4 is adjusted, as appropriate. For example, if the business discovers that it did not account for VAT payable to HMRC of £100 on a supply made in the past, and also did not account for £60 VAT reclaimable on a purchase, it should add £40 to the Box 1 figure on the current VAT Return.

How to separately declare an error to HMRC: Method 2

For certain errors a separate declaration is required to the relevant HMRC VAT Error Correction Team in writing about the mistake. The simplest way to tell them is to use Form VAT 652 "Notification of Errors in VAT Returns", which is for reporting errors on previous returns, but the business does not have to use Form VAT 652 - it can simply write a letter instead.

Businesses may, if they wish, use this method for errors of any size, even those which are below the error reporting threshold i.e. instead of a Method 1 error correction. Using this method means the business must not make adjustment for the same errors on a later VAT Return.

Method 2 must always be used if the net error exceeds the error reporting threshold or if the errors made on previous returns were made deliberately.

Surcharges, penalties and assessments

Surcharges for missed VAT Return or VAT payment deadlines

VAT-registered businesses must submit a VAT Return and pay any VAT by the relevant due date. If HMRC receives a return or VAT payment after the due date, the business is 'in default' and may have to pay a surcharge in addition to the VAT that is owed.

The first default is dealt with by a warning known as a 'Surcharge Liability Notice'. This notice tells the business that if it submits or pays late ('defaults') again during the following 12 months - known as the surcharge period - it may be charged a surcharge.

Submitting or paying late again during the surcharge period could result in a 'default surcharge'. This is a percentage of any unpaid VAT owed. Where a correct return is not submitted at all, HMRC will estimate the amount of VAT owed and base the surcharge on that amount (this is known as an assessment – see below).

HMRC assessments

Businesses have a legal obligation to submit VAT Returns and pay any VAT owed to HMRC by the relevant due date. If they do not submit a return, HMRC can issue an assessment which shows the amount of VAT that HMRC believes it is owed, based on HMRC's best estimate.

Penalties for careless and deliberate errors

Careless and deliberate errors will be liable to a penalty, whether they are adjusted on the VAT Return or separately declared.

If a business discovers an error which is neither careless nor deliberate, HMRC expects that it will take steps to adjust or declare it, as appropriate. If the business fails to take such steps, the inaccuracy will be treated as careless and a penalty will be due.

Penalties for inaccurate returns

Penalties may be applied if a VAT Return is inaccurate, and correcting this means tax is unpaid, understated, over-claimed or under-assessed. Telling HMRC about inaccuracies as soon as the business is aware of them may reduce any penalty that is due, in some cases to zero.

Penalty for late registration

Failure to register for VAT with HMRC at the right time may make a business liable to a late registration penalty.

Penalty for failure to disclose business changes

A business which undergoes a change which either cancels the existing registration or otherwise alters the registration details will face a civil penalty if it fails to disclose the changes to HMRC within 30 days of the change.

Finding out more information about VAT

Most questions can be answered by referring to the VAT section of the HMRC website.

VAT Enquiries Helpline

If the answer to a question is not on the HMRC website, the quickest and easiest way is to ring the VAT Enquiries Helpline where most VAT questions can be answered.

Letters to HMRC

The VAT General Enquiries helpline can answer most questions relating to VAT, but there may be times when it is more appropriate to write to HMRC.

This would apply if:
- the VAT information published by HMRC - either on the website or in printed notices and information sheets - has not answered a question
- the VAT General Enquiries helpline has advised the business to write
- there is real doubt about how VAT affects a particular transaction, personal situation or business

If HMRC already publishes information that answers the question, their response will give the relevant details.

Visits by VAT officers

On a control visit to a business a VAT officer can examine VAT records to make sure that they are up to date. They also check that amounts claimed from or paid to the government are correct.

INDEX